CAMBRIDGE PRIMARY
Mathematics

Skills Builder

Name:

6

Contents

Mary Wood

CAMBRIDGE
UNIVERSITY

CAMBRIDGE
UNIVERSITY PRESS

University Printing House, Cambridge CB2 8BS, United Kingdom

Cambridge University Press is part of the University of Cambridge.

It furthers the University's mission by disseminating knowledge in the pursuit of education, learning and research at the highest international levels of excellence.

www.cambridge.org
Information on this title: education.cambridge.org/9781316509180

© Cambridge University Press 2016

First published 2016

Printed in Poland by Opolgraf

A catalogue record for this publication is available from the British Library

ISBN 978-1-316-50918-0 Paperback

This book is part of the Cambridge Primary Maths project. This is an innovative combination of curriculum and resources designed to support teachers and learners to succeed in primary mathematics through best-practice international maths teaching and a problem-solving approach.

To get involved, visit
www.cie.org.uk/cambridgeprimarymaths.

Introduction

This *Skills Builder activity book* is part of a series of 12 write-in activity books for primary mathematics grades 1–6. It can be used as a standalone book, but the content also complements *Cambridge Primary Maths*. Learners progress at different rates, so this series provides a Skills Builder and a Challenge Activity Book for each Primary Mathematics Curriculum Framework Stage to support and broaden the depth of learning.

The *Skills Builder* books consolidate the learning already covered in the classroom, but provide extra support by giving short reminders of key information, topic vocabulary and hints on how best to develop maths skills and knowledge. They have also been written to support learners whose first language is not English.

How to use the books

The activities are for use by learners in school or at home, ideally with adult support. Topics have been carefully chosen to focus on those common areas where learners might need extra support. The approach is linked directly to *Cambridge Primary Maths*, but teachers and parents can pick and choose which activities to cover, or go through the books in sequence.

The varied set of activities grow in challenge through each unit, including:

- closed questions with answers, so progress can be checked
- questions with more than one possible answer
- activities requiring resources, for example, dice, spinners or digit cards
- activities and games best done with someone else, for example, in class or at home, which give the opportunity to be fully involved in the child's learning
- activities to support different learning styles: working individually, in pairs, in groups.

How to approach the activities

Space is provided for learners to write their answers in the book. Some activities might need further practice or writing, so students could be given a blank notebook at the start of the year to use alongside the book. Each activity follows a standard structure.

- **Remember** gives an overview of key learning points. They introduce core concepts and, later, can be used as a revision guide. These sections should be read with an adult who can check that the learner understands the material before attempting the activities.
- **Vocabulary** assists with difficult mathematical terms, particularly when English is not the learner's first language. Learners should read through the key vocabulary. Where necessary, they should be encouraged to clarify their understanding by using a mathematical dictionary or, ideally, by seeking adult help.

- **Hints** prompt and assist in building understanding, and steer the learner in the right direction.
- **You will need** gives learners, teachers and parents a list of resources for each activity.
- **Photocopiable resources** are provided at the end of the book, for easy assembly in class or at home.
- **Links** to the Cambridge International Examinations Primary Mathematics Curriculum Framework objectives and the corresponding *Cambridge Primary Mathematics Teacher's Resource* are given in the footnote on every page.
- **Calculators** should be used to help learners understand numbers and the number system, including place value and properties of numbers. From Stage 5, learners are expected to become proficient in using calculators in appropriate situations. This book develops the learner's knowledge of number without a calculator, although calculators can be useful for checking work.

Note:

When a 'spinner' is included, put a paperclip flat on the page so the end is over the centre of the spinner. Place the pencil point in the centre of the spinner, through the paperclip. Hold the pencil firmly and spin the paperclip to generate a result.

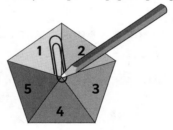

Tracking progress

Answers to closed questions are given at the back of the book; these allow teachers, parents and learners to check their work.

When completing each activity, teachers and parents are advised to encourage self-assessment by asking the students how straightforward they found the activity. When learners are reflecting on games, they should consider how challenging the mathematics was, not who won. Learners could use a ✓/ ✗ or red/green colouring system to record their self-assessment for each activity.

These assessments provide teachers and parents with an understanding of how best to support individual learners' next steps.

Place value, ordering and rounding (whole numbers)

Remember

Place value

The ten digits 0, 1, 2, 3, 4, 5, 6, 7, 8 and 9 are used to build up numbers.

M	HTh	TTh	Th	H	T	U
1	0	0	0	0	0	0

Read as one million.

Multiplying and dividing by 10 and 100

When you **multiply** numbers by 10 / 100 / 1000 all the digits move 1 / 2 / 3 places to the **left**.

When you **divide** numbers by 10 / 100 / 1000 all the digits move 1 / 2 / 3 places to the **right**.

Comparing numbers

= means **is equal to**, < means **is less than** and > means **is greater than**.

Rounding numbers

When rounding to the nearest 10 look at the units digit, when rounding to the nearest 100 look at the tens digit and when rounding to the nearest 1000 look at the hundreds digit, so 8364 rounds down to 8000.

Positioning numbers on a blank number line
Example:

Draw an arrow to mark the position of 3500 on the blank number line.

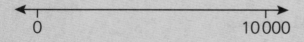

Answer:

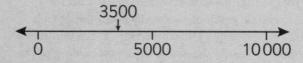

It is helpful to mark 5000 halfway along the line.

1 Here is a place-value chart.

100 000	200 000	300 000	400 000	500 000	600 000	700 000	800 000	900 000
10 000	20 000	30 000	40 000	50 000	60 000	70 000	80 000	90 000
1000	2000	3000	4000	5000	6000	7000	8000	9000
100	200	300	400	500	600	700	800	900
10	20	30	40	50	60	70	80	90
1	2	3	4	5	6	7	8	9

What number is represented on the chart?
Write the number in words and in figures. _____

_____

What does the digit 6 represent in the number 654 321? _____

> **Hint:** You will need to write 6 followed by one of:
> hundred thousand, ten thousand, thousand, hundred, tens, units

2 Here are four numbers.

9009   90 009

9 000 009   9 000 009

Circle the number ninety thousand and nine.

3 Complete each calculation.

☐ × 1000 = 35 000   ☐ ÷ 1000 = 606

68 000 ÷ ☐ = 68   10 100 ÷ ☐ = 101

☐ × 100 = 480 000   ☐ × 100 = 90 100

4 Complete this table to show the numbers rounded to the nearest 1000.

	rounded to the nearest 1000
515	
5151	
51 515	
515 151	

Unit 1A: Number and problem solving
CPM framework 6Nn2, 6Nn4, 6Nn8, 6Nn10, 6Nn12, 6Nn13; Teacher's Resource 1.1, 1.2, 3.1

9

5   Circle the number that is nearest to 10 000.

10 060   11 000   9960   9909

> **Hint:** The number could be greater or less than 10 000.

6   Find your height, in millimetres.

Round to the nearest 10 mm.   _____

Round to the nearest 100 mm.   _____

Round to the nearest 1000 mm.   _____

7   Use the digits 3, 4, 5 and 6 to make the four-digit number that is nearest to 4000.

8   Use one of the signs <, > or = to make these number sentences correct.

5 × 1000 ☐ 50 000 ÷ 10

5005 ☐ 50 000 ÷ 10

500 × 1000 ☐ 1 million

9   Estimate the number marked by the arrow on the number line.

0   10 000

10   This number line is from zero to one million.
Write the letter of the arrow that points to the number 50 000. _____

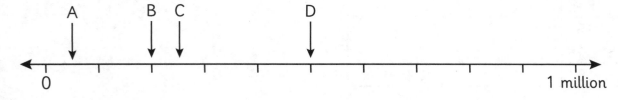

A   B   C   D

0   1 million

Multiples, factors, odd and even numbers

Remember

Finding common multiples

List the **multiples**, then inspect the lists to find the common multiples.

Example: Find common multiples of 4 and 5:
Multiples of 4: 4, 8, 12, 16, **20**, 24, 28, 32, 36, **40** …
Multiples of 5: 5, 10, 15, **20**, 25, 30, 35, **40** …

20 and 40 are **common multiples** of 4 and 5. 20 is the **lowest common multiple** of 4 and 5.

A **general statement** is a rule that always works.

You might be asked to find examples that match a general statement or find a counter-example to show that a statement is false.

Example: The sum of three odd numbers is always odd.
Particular case: 1 + 3 + 5 = 9
General case: odd + odd + odd = odd

You will need: a set of 1–10 number cards and a set of target number cards from Resource 1, page 81, for activity 2; a set of 1–10 number cards for activity 3; keep the additional 0 and 5 cards for Unit 15

Vocabulary

odd, even, multiple, common multiple, factor, general statement, product, prime number

1   You can use a factor tree to find factors of two-digit numbers, for example:

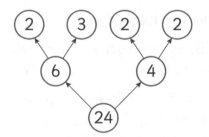

Hint: Be careful not to confuse **factors** with **multiples**. Use a dictionary to check the meaning of mathematical words if you are unsure.

You know you have completed the factorisation when the numbers on the top row are all prime numbers.

Build up factor trees for these numbers.

18   20   32

36   40   48

2 Finding factors – a game for two players

Use the 1–10 number cards and target number cards:

12	14	15	16	18	20	21	24

25	27	30	32	36	40	42

Shuffle the target cards and place them face down in a pile. Shuffle and share out the 1–10 number cards between the players. Turn over the first target card. Each player looks at their number cards to see if they have a card that is a factor of the target number; if so they put it down in front of them. Players can only play one card each turn. Play continues until one player has laid down all their number cards. This player is the winner.

> **Hint:** You have drawn factor trees for some of the target numbers in activity 1.
> You might find it useful to draw factor trees for the other numbers.
> Some of the 1–10 cards are more useful than others.
> Which is a useful card to have?

3 Odd and evens – a game for two players

Players are designated A and B. Each player shuffles their 1–10 number cards and places them face down in a pile.

Both players turn over the top card from their pile. If the product is even player A gets a point, if the product is odd player B gets a point. The first player to 10 points wins the game.

> **Hint:** Would you rather be player A or player B?

Look at the results for some of the calculations.
The even products are shaded.

Complete these general statements about the products of odd and even numbers:

odd × odd = _____

odd × even or even × odd = _____

even × even = _____

×	1	2	3	4
1	1	2	3	4
2	2	4	6	8
3	3	6	9	12
4	4	8	12	16

4 The example shows a way of finding
common multiples by writing the first ten
multiples for each pair of numbers, then
circling the common multiples.

4	6
4	6
8	(12)
(12)	18
16	(24)
20	30
(24)	(36)
28	42
32	48
(36)	54
40	60

Draw similar diagrams for these pairs of numbers.

2	5

3	4

4	7

3	10

Prime numbers

Vocabulary
prime number, factor

Remember

A prime number has exactly two factors.

NOTE: 1 is **not** a prime number. It has only one factor (1)

Examples of prime numbers: 2, 3, 5, 7, 11, 13, 17, 19

1 Here is a number grid from 1 to 100.

1	2	3	4	5	6	7	8	9	10
11	12	13	14	15	16	17	18	19	20
21	22	23	24	25	26	27	28	29	30
31	32	33	34	35	36	37	38	39	40
41	42	43	44	45	46	47	48	49	50
51	52	53	54	55	56	57	58	59	60
61	62	63	64	65	66	67	68	69	70
71	72	73	74	75	76	77	78	79	80
81	82	83	84	85	86	87	88	89	90
91	92	93	94	95	96	97	98	99	100

Use the grid. Follow these instructions.

- Cross out the number 1.

- Shade in all the multiples of 2 except 2.

- What do you notice? Can you explain what you see?

- Shade in all the multiples of 3 except 3.

- Some numbers had already been crossed out.
  Which ones?

- Shade all the multiples of 5 except 5, then 7 except 7.
  What do you notice?

Now look at your grid. What is special about the numbers
that you have not crossed out?

The process you have followed is known as the Sieve of
Eratosthenes after the Greek mathematician who first used
the idea to find prime numbers up to 100.

Unit 1A: Number and problem solving
CPM framework 6Nn19, 6Ps9; Teacher's Resource 2.3

2 Find two different prime numbers that total 9.

☐ + ☐ = 9

Find two different prime numbers that total 16.

☐ + ☐ = 16

3 Use the clues to find the two prime numbers less than 20.

Prime number 1: This prime number added to 3 is a multiple of 8. _____

Prime number 2: This prime number is one more than a multiple of 4. _____

> **Hint:** Try listing all the prime numbers less than 20 and cross out the ones that do not satisfy the clue.

4 Shade all the prime numbers in this grid.

What letter is revealed? _____

14	2	13	5	8
15	3	1	11	15
1	11	19	7	6
9	17	9	15	12
12	5	16	4	14

5 Draw a path between the two shaded numbers on this grid.
You may pass **only** through prime numbers.

You must not move diagonally.

2	4	6	8	13
3	13	19	17	15
1	11	15	7	5
15	12	5	1	2
11	14	16	4	11

Multiplication strategies

You will need:
counters for
activity 3

Vocabulary
multiple, near
multiple of 10

Remember

Multiplication strategies

You should learn and remember some mathematical facts, for example. multiplication facts up to 10×10.

You can use these facts to work mentally. You can use strategies such as:

- using place value and multiplication facts
- multiplying pairs of multiples of 10
- multiplying near multiples of 10 by multiplying by the multiple and adjusting
- multiplying by halving one number and doubling the other.

Practise these strategies using the examples in this unit.

1 Using place value and multiplication facts

Examples:
$$0.8 \times 7 = (8 \div 10) \times 7$$
$$= (8 \times 7) \div 10$$
$$= 56 \div 10$$
$$= 5.6$$

$$4.8 \div 6 = (48 \div 10) \div 6$$
$$= (48 \div 6) \div 10$$
$$= 8 \div 10$$
$$= 0.8$$

Now try these.

$0.9 \times 8 =$ $0.6 \times 7 =$

$6.3 \div 9 =$ $5.6 \div 8 =$

2 Multiplying pairs of multiples of 10

Examples: I know that $3 \times 4 = 12$

so $30 \times 40 = 1200$

I know that $6 \times 4 = 24$

so $600 \times 40 = 24\,000$

Now try these.

$70 \times 80 =$ $40 \times 90 =$

$300 \times 70 =$ $400 \times 60 =$

Unit 1A: Number and problem solving
CPM framework 6Nc7, 6Nc8, 6Nc14, 6Nc15, 6Nc16, 6Pt1, 6Ps1; Teacher's Resource 3.2

3 Three in a row – a game for two players

Use counters or cross out the numbers on the grid.

Take turns to choose a calculation to work out.

Say which you are working on and find the answer on the grid.

Put a counter on the answer.

The winner is the first to get three in a row.

Calculations

30 × 60	30 × 50	50 × 40	40 × 60
30 × 600	30 × 500	50 × 400	40 × 600
300 × 60	300 × 50	500 × 40	400 × 60
300 × 600	300 × 500	500 × 400	400 × 600

2000	200 000	15 000	18 000
24 000	18 000	2400	1500
15 000	24 000	20 000	1800
240 000	180 000	150 000	20 000

Hint: Some numbers are repeated on the grid, for example 15 000 which is the answer to 30 × 500 and 300 × 50.

4 Multiplying near multiples of 10 by multiplying by the multiple and adjusting

Examples:
$$16 \times 51 = (16 \times 50) + 16 \qquad 16 \times 49 = (16 \times 50) - 16$$
$$= 800 + 16 \qquad\qquad\qquad = 800 - 16$$
$$= 816 \qquad\qquad\qquad\qquad = 784$$

Now try these.

$17 \times 41 =$ $17 \times 39 =$

$14 \times 29 =$ $14 \times 31 =$

Hint: Show the stages in your working as some test questions require the working in addition to the answer.

Unit 1A: Number and problem solving
CPM framework 6Nc7, 6Nc8, 6Nc14, 6Nc15, 6Nc16, 6Pt1, 6Ps1; Teacher's Resource 3.2

13

5 Multiplying by halving one number and doubling the other

Examples

16 × 5 is equivalent to 8 × 10 = 80   7 × 8 = 56
15 × 18 is equivalent to 30 × 9 = 270   so 14 × 4 = 56
                                                                    and 28 × 2 = 56

Now try these.

25 × 14 =   45 × 16 =

35 × 24 =   15 × 14 =

Write a set of related facts, starting with 9 × 8 = 72

_____   _____   _____

Write a set of related facts, starting with 3 × 16 = 48

_____   _____   _____

6 Circle each multiplication that gives the answer 2400.

60 × 400   40 × 60   80 × 300   20 × 120

7 Complete this number sentence.

35 × 8 = ☐ × 2   11 × 16 = ☐ × 4

8 Use the fact that 6 × 7 = 42 to complete the diagram.

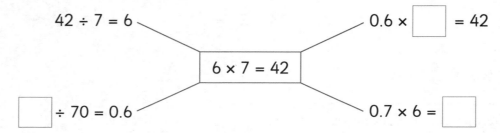

42 ÷ 7 = 6   0.6 × ☐ = 42

6 × 7 = 42

☐ ÷ 70 = 0.6   0.7 × 6 = ☐

Unit 1A: Number and problem solving
CPM framework 6Nc7, 6Nc8, 6Nc14, 6Nc15, 6Nc16, 6Pt1, 6Ps1; Teacher's Resource 3.2

Number sequences

Remember

The numbers in a **sequence** are called terms.

To work out the rule or pattern for a sequence, look at the differences between **consecutive** terms.

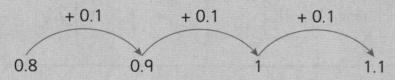

The pattern or rule is + 0.1

Vocabulary
sequence, rule, term

1   A sequence starts at 300 and 40 is subtracted each time.

300   260   220   180   ...

What is the first number in the sequence that is less than zero? _____

2   Write the next two numbers in each sequence.

1.5, 1.6, 1.7, 1.8, 1.9, ☐ , ☐

$\frac{1}{2}$, 1, $1\frac{1}{2}$, 2, $2\frac{1}{2}$, ☐ , ☐

1007, 1005, 1003, 1001, ☐ , ☐

3   Work with a partner for this activity.

Write a sequence where the terms:
* are multiples of 3
* are odd numbers
* are multiples of 6
* include 25 and 33.

Swap sequences with your partner and ask them to identify the rule you used.
Agree on the rule and record your results.

Start number	Rule	Number of terms	Sequence

4 The numbers in this sequence increase by 3 each time.   3, 6, 9, 12 …

The numbers in this sequence increase by 7 each time.   7, 14, 21, 28 …

What is the smallest number that is in both sequences?   _____

5 Alana makes a sequence of numbers.
Her rule is to add the same amount each time.

Write the missing numbers.

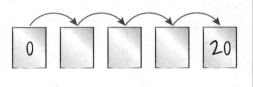

> **Hint:** If you do not recognise
> the sequence, use this method.
> Number of jumps = 4
> Difference between largest and smallest number = 20
> 20 ÷ 4 = 5 so rule is +5

6 The numbers in these sequences
increase by the same amount each time.
Find the missing numbers.

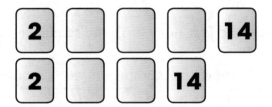

7 Here is part of a number grid.

1	2	3	4
5	6	7	8
9	10	11	12
13	14	15	16

Here is another part of the same grid.

Write the missing number.

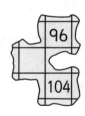

8 Here is a sequence made from circles. The sequence continues in the same way.
Draw the next two diagrams.

pattern   pattern   pattern   pattern
  1   2   3   4

Complete the table.

Pattern number	1	2	3	4	5	6	7	8	9	10
Number of circles	2	4								

What is the rule for the sequence? _____

Unit 1A: Number and problem solving
CPM framework 6Nn1, 6Nn15, 6Ps3; Teacher's Resource 4.3

Drawing and measuring lines and angles

Remember

When **drawing lines and angles**, take care to position the ruler or protractor carefully and always count from zero.

Lines are measured in **centimetres** (cm) or **millimetres** (mm).

You will need:
ruler,
protractor

Angles are measured in **degrees** (°).

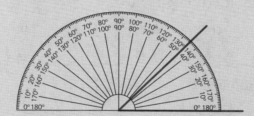

This angle is 45°.

---

1 Here is a right-angled triangle.

Measure the shortest side in **centimetres**. _____

Measure the longest side in **millimetres**. _____

Measure the two acute angles. _____ _____

Find the sum of the two angles. _____

> **Hint:** The sum of the two angles should be 90°.

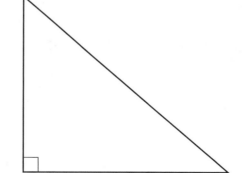

2 Draw a new line 4 centimetres longer than this line.

_____

Unit 1B: Measure and problem solving, Unit 3C: Geometry and problem solving
CPM framework 6MI4, 6Nn16, 6Gs5, 6Pt2; Teacher's Resource 5.2, 35.1

17

3 Measure the angles marked *a*, *b* and *c*.

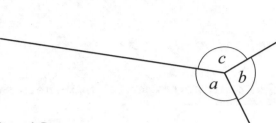

4 Here are four lines labelled A, B, C and D.

A ————————————————————

B ————————————————————

C ——————————————————————

D ——————————————

Measure the length of each line.
Write your answer in millimetres and in centimetres.

A _____mm _____cm   B _____mm _____cm

C _____mm _____cm   D _____mm _____cm

Draw a straight line 3 cm shorter than line C.

Draw a different line 4 cm longer than line D.

5 Draw each of these angles.
50° 100° 135° 75°

Unit 1B: Measure and problem solving, **Unit 3C:** Geometry and problem solving
CPM framework 6MI4, 6Nn16, 6Gs5, 6Pt2; Teacher's Resource 5.2, 35.1

Angles

Remember

Types of angle

90° is a right angle

acute angles are less than 90°

obtuse angles are more than 90°

a straight line is 180°

Calculating angles

Angles at a point
$a + b + c = 360°$

c a b

Angles in a triangle
$a + b + c = 180°$

c a b

1 Draw and cut out a triangle. Tear off the three corners and rearrange them to make a straight line.

What is the sum of the three angles? _____

> **Hint:** The sum of angles on a straight line = the sum of angles in a triangle.

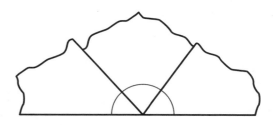

2 Find the size of each angle marked with a letter.
The diagrams are not drawn accurately.

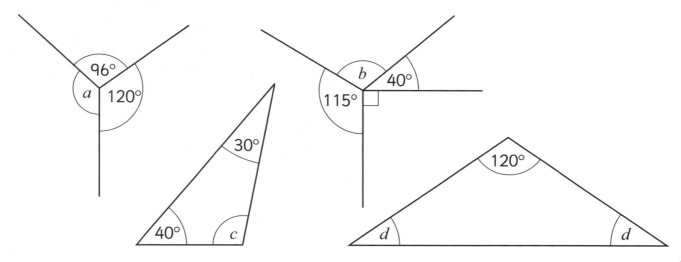

3 Drawing and estimating the size of angles in a triangle
   – an activity for pairs

Player 1 draws a triangle and labels the
vertices A, B and C.

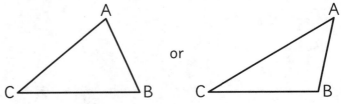

Both players estimate the size of the three
angles and record their measurements.

Players measure the size of the angles and compare them with their estimates.
For each angle, the player with the closer estimate scores 1 point.
The winner is the player with more points after five rounds.

Record two of your results here:

Draw your triangle here:

	Angle size			
	Player 1		Player 2	
	E	M	E	M
Angle 1				
Angle 2				
Angle 3				

E is the estimated angle
M is the measured angle

Draw your triangle here:

	Angle size			
	Player 1		Player 2	
	E	M	E	M
Angle 1				
Angle 2				
Angle 3				

E is the estimated angle
M is the measured angle

Unit 1C: Geometry and problem solving
CPM framework 6Gs5, 6Gs6, 6Ps5; Teacher's Resource 9.1

Transformations on a grid

Remember

Draw the **reflection** of a simple shape in a mirror line touching it at one point, where the edges of the shape are not necessarily parallel or perpendicular to the mirror line.

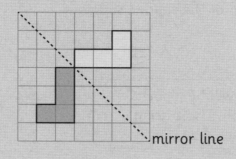
mirror line

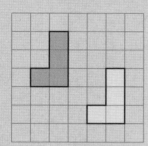

Draw the position of a simple shape after it has been **translated**, for example 3 units to the right and 2 units down.

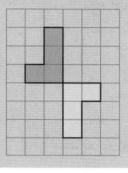

Draw the position of a simple shape after a **rotation** of 90° or 180° about a vertex.

---

1 The quadrilateral is translated so that point A moves to point B.

Draw the quadrilateral in its new position.

> **Hint:** The shape remains exactly the same. You may find it useful to draw the shape on tracing paper and then move it on the grid.

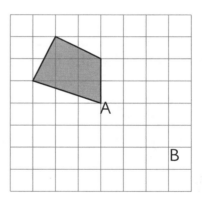

2 Describe the **translation** that moves shape A to shape B.

_____

_____

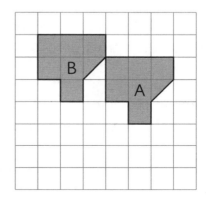

> **Hint:** Describe the movement across the page first, and up or down second.

3 Draw the reflection of the shaded shape in the mirror line.

> **Hint:** The shape will be flipped over in a reflection. Use tracing paper to help you.

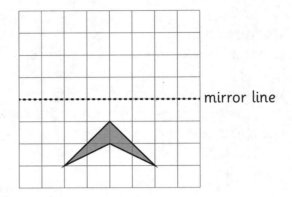

mirror line

4 Draw two more circles on the grid to make a design that has a **line of symmetry**.

> **Hint: Mirror lines** may be vertical, horizontal or diagonal.

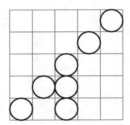

5 Here is a shaded shape drawn on a square grid.

The shape is rotated 180° about point A.

Draw the shape in its new position on the grid.

> **Hint:** Using tracing paper also helps with rotation.
> - Copy the shape.
> - Place it on top of the original shape, put a pencil through the cross and turn the tracing paper through 180° to give the new position.

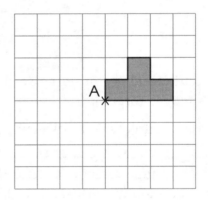

6 This shape is rotated through 90° clockwise about the point marked with a cross.

Draw a ring around the diagram that shows the correct position of the rotated shape.

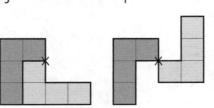
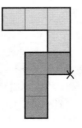
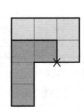

Unit 1C: Geometry and problem solving
CPM framework 6Gp2; Teacher's Resource 10.1, 10.2, 10.3

3D shapes

Remember

The shape of the two parallel faces gives the **prism** its name.
Cubes and cuboids are special types of prism.

cube

triangular prism

hexagonal prism

The shape of the base gives the **pyramid** its name.
The other faces are always triangular.

square-based
pyramid

triangular-based
pyramid or tetrahedron

hexagonal-based
pyramid

The **net of a solid** is what it looks like when opened out flat. The nets
of prisms will always have two identical faces; the nets of pyramids will
have a base shape and all other faces will be triangles.

1   The net of a cube is constructed from
6 square faces.
It can be folded to form a cube.

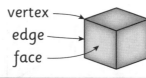

Number of faces	Number of vertices	Number of edges
6	8	12

Pedro makes two solids from
equilateral triangles.

Complete the table showing
the properties of these solids.

octahedron

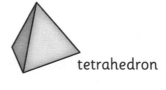

tetrahedron

	Number of faces	Number of vertices	Number of edges
tetrahedron			
octahedron			

Hint: When you are using a picture to help you count the number of faces,
edges and vertices remember that some are hidden from view.

Unit 1C: Number and problem solving, Unit 3C: Geometry and problem solving
CPM framework 6Gs2, 6Gs4, 6Pt4; Teacher's Resource 8.2, 8.3, 33.1, 33.2

23

2 Here is information about a three-dimensional shape.

Number of faces	Number of vertices	Number of edges
5	5	8

Circle one name to identify the shape.

triangular prism   triangular-based pyramid   square-based pyramid   pentagonal prism

3 Fatima makes a model of a prism.

Which one of these nets could she use? _____

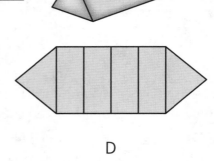

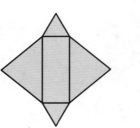
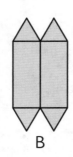
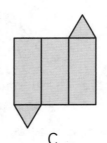

A   B   C   D

4 Here is **part** of a net for a different triangular prism.

Use the grid to complete
the drawing of the net.

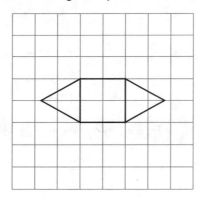

5 Here is the net of a 3D solid.

The net is folded to make a solid.

Look at the edge marked A on the net.
Write B on the edge that it joins to when
the net is folded up.

What is the name of the solid?

_____

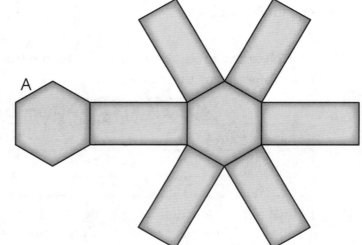

Unit 1C: Number and problem solving, Unit 3C: Geometry and problem solving
CPM framework 6Gs2, 6Gs4, 6Pt4; Teacher's Resource 8.2, 8.3, 33.1, 33.2

Numbers in Ancient Greece

Pythagoras was born about 580 BC on the small island of Samos in the Aegean Sea. He was an outstanding mathematical thinker who founded an academy. He taught orally and did not write down his ideas but it is known that he and his fellow mathematicians laid down the foundations of number theory and computation.

The Pythagoreans were fascinated by the geometrical shapes that they could make using numbers of pebbles or dots drawn in the sand, for example triangular numbers, square numbers and the relationships between them.

These are the triangular numbers:

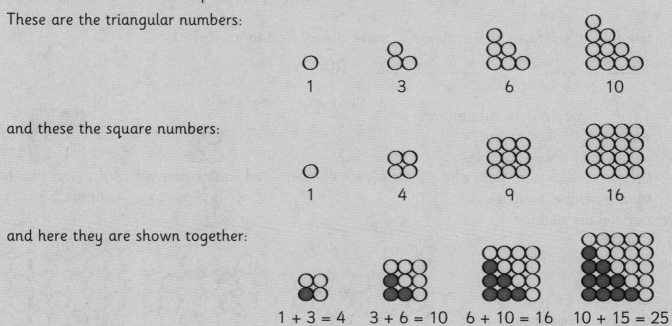

and these the square numbers:

and here they are shown together:

$1 + 3 = 4$ $3 + 6 = 10$ $6 + 10 = 16$ $10 + 15 = 25$

Answer these questions on triangular and square numbers.

1 Draw the next pattern in each of the three sequences above.

2 Find the missing number in this number sequence.

1, 3, 6, 10, _____ , 21

3 List the square numbers up to 100.

_____

4 Jodi is thinking of a square number.

She rounds it to the nearest ten.

Her answer is 20.

What number is she thinking of? _____

Unit 2A: Number and problem solving, Unit 3A: Number and problem solving
CPM framework 6Nn15, 6Nn20, 6Ps3, 6Ps9; Teacher's Resource 11.2, 23.2

25

5 Olly uses cubes to make a pattern.

 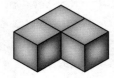 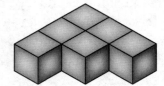 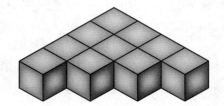

How many cubes will he need to make the next model in his sequence? _____

6 Use four different square numbers to make these calculations correct.

_____ + _____ = 10   _____ + _____ = 20

7 The Pythagoreans found patterns when they looked at the numbers of dots or pebbles they needed to add on to one square number to make the next square number.

O

1st square number   2nd square number   3rd square number
                              needs 3 more   needs 5 more

Colour the patterns for the next seven square numbers, then complete the table.

 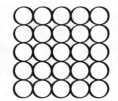 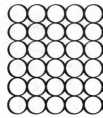 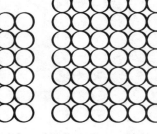

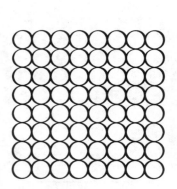 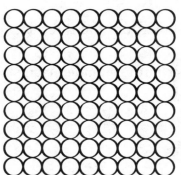 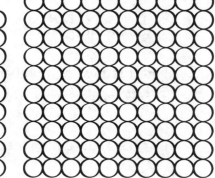

What patterns can you see? _____

Square number	1	2	3	4	5	6	7	8	9	10
Number of dots	1	4	9	16						100
Number of dots added		3								

Unit 2A: Number and problem solving, **Unit 3A:** Number and problem solving
CPM framework 6Nn15, 6Nn20, 6Ps3, 6Ps9; Teacher's Resource 11.2, 23.2

The decimal system

You will need:
counters for activity 5, resource 2, page 82, for activity 6

Vocabulary
tenth, hundredth

Remember

Place value
The position of a digit in a number gives its value. The **decimal point** separates whole numbers from decimal places.

T	U	t	h
5	7	0	8

Read as fifty-seven point zero eight.

Multiplying and dividing by 10 and 100
Use the same rules as those used for whole numbers (see page 4).
Examples: $356 \div 100 = 3.56$ $4.7 \times 10 = 47$

Rounding numbers
When rounding to the nearest tenth look at the hundredths digit, for example 46.45 is 46.5 to the nearest tenth.

When rounding to the nearest whole number look at the tenths digit, for example 46.45 is 46 to the nearest whole number.

Ordering decimals
Example: Order the numbers 5.22, 2.5, 0.52, 2.05, 5.02 starting with the smallest number.

Start by writing all numbers with the **same** number of decimal places (Write 2.5 as 2.50) then look at the digit with the highest place value, in this case units, then look at the tenths to give:
0.52   2.05   2.50   5.02   5.22

---

1   What does the digit 7 in 3.75 represent? _____

What does the digit 5 represent? _____

> **Hint:** You must give the numerical value and the place value in your answer.

2   **Place value challenge – a game for two players**

Take turns to spin the spinner and write your number in any cell on the game board. The winner is the player with the higher number when all the boxes have been filled.

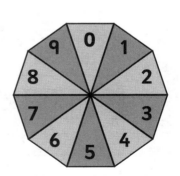

Game 1

	H	T	U	t	h
Player 1					
Player 2					

Game 2

	H	T	U	t	h
Player 1					
Player 2					

3 Complete the table. Use the numbers from question 2.

Number	Number rounded to the nearest tenth	Number rounded to the nearest whole number

4 Round 1.355 metres to the nearest metre. _____

Round $5.39 to the nearest 10 cents. _____

> **Hint:** This is another way of saying 'round to the nearest tenth'.

5 Multiplying and dividing decimals – a game for two players

Each player will need counters (or you could cross out the numbers in the grid) and a copy of the grid.

0.65	540	38	1	5.4
94	100	0.07	380	65
0.94	0.38	70	700	0.54
650	5400	0.1	940	1000

Numbers					
10	54	6.5	3.8	0.7	9.4

Operations			
× 10	× 100	÷ 10	÷ 100

Take turns to choose a number and an operation and work out the answer.

If your partner agrees with your answer you put one of your counters on the answer in the grid.

The winner is the first to get three in a row.

Unit 2A: Number and problem solving
CPM framework 6Nn3, 6Nn5, 6Nn9, 6Nn14, 6Nn16; Teacher's Resource 12.1, 12.3

6 Ordering decimals – a game for two players

Shuffle the cards from the resource and place them face down.

Turn over the top card.

Players decide in which box of the first row of boxes to place the number.

Continue to fill in the other three boxes.

The aim is to write the four numbers in order, from smallest to largest.

The winner of the round is the player whose numbers are written in order or who has more numbers in the correct order.

Play 5 rounds.

Player 1   **Player 2**

Round 1 [ ] [ ] [ ] [ ]   [ ] [ ] [ ] [ ]

Winner _____

Round 2 [ ] [ ] [ ] [ ]   [ ] [ ] [ ] [ ]

Winner _____

Round 3 [ ] [ ] [ ] [ ]   [ ] [ ] [ ] [ ]

Winner _____

Round 4 [ ] [ ] [ ] [ ]   [ ] [ ] [ ] [ ]

Winner _____

Round 5 [ ] [ ] [ ] [ ]   [ ] [ ] [ ] [ ]

Winner _____

Addition and subtraction of decimals

Remember

Addition of decimals

You will need: resource 3, page 83, for activity 2

```
  3 6.7           3 6.7                          3 6.7
+ 1 8.5         + 1 8.5                        + 1 8.5
───────   ⟶       4 0.0   30 + 10     ⟶         5 5.2
                  1 4.0    6 + 8                  1   1
                    1.2    0.7 + 0.5
                ───────
                  5 5.2
```

Subtraction of decimals

```
  3 2.5           20  + 11  + 1.5                ² ³²·¹2.⁵5
−   5.8     ⟶   −            5     0.8      ⟶    −   5.8
───────         ───────────────────             ───────
                  20  +  6  + 0.7                  2 6.7
```

1   Here are five number discs.

(0.1) (0.2) (0.3) (0.4) (0.5)

Use each disc once to make the total along each line 1.

> **Hint:** If you find problems of this type challenging try cutting out discs and placing them on the grid. It is quicker than crossing out or rubbing out!

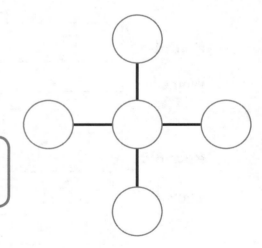

2   **Sum to 10 – a game for 2–4 players**

Place the cards from resource 3 in a random order, face down on the table. Players take turns to pick up two differently sized cards. If the cards make a correct sum the player keeps the cards, otherwise the cards are replaced in their original position on the table. The winner is the player with the most matching pairs.

Complete these missing number problems.

4.6 + ☐ = 10   5.86 + ☐ = 10

8.1 + ☐ = 10   3.62 + ☐ = 10

Unit 2A: Number and problem solving
CPM framework 6Nc1, 6Nc2, 6Nc9, 6Nc11, 6Nc12, 6Pt1, 6Ps1; Teacher's Resource 12.2, 12.3

3 Find the pairs that total 1 on this grid.

0.51	0.26	0.37	0.74	5.4
0.92	0.08	0.75	0.89	65
0.24	0.19	0.63	0.25	0.54
0.11	0.81	0.49	0.76	1000

Hint: Make a similar grid and challenge a friend to find the pairs.

4 Look at this example that shows how you can start with doubling 78 and derive double 7.8 or double 0.78.

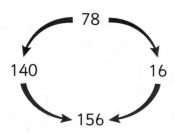

Double 7.8 = 15.6 (double 78 ÷ 10 = 156 ÷ 10 = 15.6)

Double 0.78 = 1.56 (double 78 ÷ 100 = 156 ÷ 100 = 1.56)

Use this method to work out the following:

- double 34, double 3.4 and double 0.34
- double 69, double 6.9 and double 0.69

5 Calculate:

63.4 + 32.5   35.8 + 12.9   12.9 + 73.4

43.9 – 21.7   34.2 – 19.4   21.8 – 19.6

Unit 2A: Number and problem solving
CPM framework 6Nc1, 6Nc2, 6Nc9, 6Nc11, 6Nc12, 6Pt1, 6Ps1; Teacher's Resource 12.2, 12.3

31

Positive and negative numbers

You will need:
resource 4,
page 84,
for activity 7

Remember

To **find the difference between positive and negative numbers**, use a number line, for example the difference between −3 and 4 is 7.

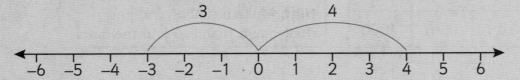

To **find the difference between two negative numbers**, use a number line, for example the difference between −1 and −5 is 4.

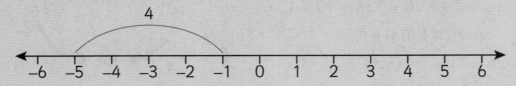

Vocabulary
positive,
negative, zero,
difference

1 Zoe and Mia record the temperature each day for a week.

0°C   1°C   −3°C   −4°C   −1°C   6°C   8°C

Put the temperatures in order of size from lowest to highest.

_____

Hint: −4°C feels colder than −3°C.

Zoe and Mia play outside when the temperature is above freezing.

- How many days did Zoe and Mia play outside? _____
- How many temperatures are below 1°C? _____
- What is the lowest temperature? _____

2 Find the difference between the numbers in each pair.

5 and −3

6 and −2

−6 and −1

−5 and 0

Hint: Use a number line to help you.

Unit 2A: Number and problem solving
CPM framework 6Nn11, 6Nc13, 6Pt2; Teacher's Resource 13.1

3   The numbers in a sequence decrease by 3 each time.

Write the missing numbers in the sequence.

8	5			

4   I count on in equal steps.

My first number is –4, my fifth number is 4.

What is my third number?

–4		?		4

I count back in equal steps.

My first number is 3, my fifth number is –3

What is my third number?

3		?		–3

5   Here is a function machine for subtracting 3.

IN → – 3 → OUT

Complete the table.

In	6	2	0	–1	–4
Out					

6   Work out these temperature problems.

- At 08:00 the temperature was 3°C.
  By 12:00 the temperature has increased by 5°.
  What was the temperature at 12:00?   _____

- The temperature rises from –11°C to –3°C
  How many degrees does it rise?   _____

- The temperature was –8°C. It rises by 12°.
  What is the new temperature?   _____

7   Compare numbers – an activity for two players

Cut out the number cards from resource 4. Place the cards on the grid on the resource so every statement is correct.

When you have both finished compare your results and sort out any errors.

Record your results.

☐ < ☐   ☐ > ☐

☐ < ☐   ☐ > ☐

☐ < ☐   ☐ > ☐

> **Hint:** It is useful to start by ordering the playing cards.

Unit 2A: Number and problem solving
CPM framework 6Nn11, 6Nc13, 6Pt2; Teacher's Resource 13.1

33

Mental strategies for addition and subtraction

Remember

Adding and subtracting near multiples of 10, 100 and 1000
You may find it helpful to imagine, or draw, the numbers on a number line and then use strategies such as:
- $3127 + 4998 = 8125$ because it is $3127 + 5000 - 2$ which is $8127 - 2$
- $5678 - 1996 = 3682$ because it is $5678 - 2000 + 4$ which is $3678 + 4$

Adding and subtracting near multiples of 1 when adding and subtracting numbers with one decimal place
You may find it helpful to imagine, or draw, the numbers on a number line and then use strategies such as:
- $5.6 + 2.9 = 8.5$ because it is $5.6 + 3 - 0.1$ which is $8.6 - 0.1$
- $13.5 - 2.1 = 11.4$ because it is $13.5 - 2 - 0.1$ which is $11.5 - 0.1$

You will need: counters for activity 4

1 Work with a partner.

Work out each calculation and record your answer. Take turns to explain your method to your partner.

Hint: Try to do the calculation in your head. If this is not possible, draw a number line or use jottings to help you.

$570 + 250 = \boxed{}$

$620 - 380 = \boxed{}$

$240 + 370 = \boxed{}$

$\boxed{} - 370 = 240$

$5.7 + 2.5 = \boxed{}$

$6.2 - 3.8 = \boxed{}$

$0.56 + 0.72 = \boxed{}$

$0.63 - 0.48 = \boxed{}$

$2.4 + 8.7 = \boxed{}$

$0.24 + \boxed{} = 0.78$

$6.1 - 2.4 = \boxed{}$

$0.95 - \boxed{} = 0.67$

Unit 2A: Number and problem solving
CPM framework 6Nc4, 6Nc5, 6Nc6, 6Pt1, 6Ps1; Teacher's Resource 14.2

2 Here are three examples of calculation strategies.

Some are correct and some are incorrect.

Mark each example with a tick (✓) if it is correct and a cross (✗) if it is incorrect. If it is incorrect write a correct version.

Calculation	Strategy	✓ or ✗	Correct version
13.4 – 6.8	13.4 – 7 – 0.2		
12.4 + 3.9	12.4 + 4 – 0.1		
31.2 – 9.9	31.2 – 10 + 0.1		

3 Gianni knows the fact: Double 3.7 is 7.4

Show how he could use **this fact** to work out 3.7 + 3.6

> **Hint:** You must show how to use the given fact.

4 Find the difference – a game for two players

Take turns to choose one number from group A and one number from group B and work out the **difference** between the two numbers. If it corresponds to a number on the game board place a counter on that square.

The winner is the first player to have four counters in a row: horizontally, vertically or diagonally.

Group A		
1006	2005	3001
4002	5004	6003

Group B		
2996	3997	4998
5998	6994	7997

3992	1996	2008	996	5998	1007
1005	5992	1990	991	2991	6
3993	5	4996	1006	4992	2992
2993	991	994	1994	996	3995
1992	6991	1997	1990	5	2997
3993	2006	5	2993	3007	4989

Divisibility rules

Remember

Divisibility rules

2   The units digit is divisible by 2.

4   The number made by the last two digits is divisible by 4.

5   The units digit is 5 or 0.

10   The units digit is 0.

25   The last two digits are 00, 25, 50 or 75.

100   The last two digits are 00.

You will need:
resource 1, page 81, for activity 3

Vocabulary
divisible

Investigating the 2 times table

The 2 times table starts:

$1 \times 2 = 2$
$2 \times 2 = 4$
$3 \times 2 = 6$
$4 \times 2 = 8$
$5 \times 2 = 10$
$6 \times 2 = 12$

The units digits of the answers are 2, 4, 6, 8, 0 and then they repeat.

Copy the units digits up to the first repeat in the box.

Start at 2 and join 2 to 4.

Join 4 to 6 (the next number in the list).

Join 6 to 8 (the next number in the list).

Join 8 to 0 (the next number in the list).

Join 0 to 2 (the last number in the list).

You should know that multiples of 2 end in 0, 2, 4, 6 or 8.
This is the divisibility rule for 2.

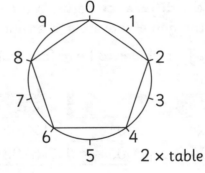

2 × table

units digit

2
4
6
8
0
2	repeat

---

1   Complete the diagram for the 5 times table.

All multiples of 5 end in 0 or 5.

Multiples of 10 are multiples of 2 and multiples of 5.
What is the units digit for all numbers divisible by 10?

_____

Hint: Remember you must focus on the units digits.

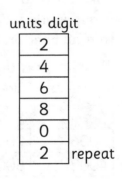

5 × table

units digit

Unit 2A: Number and problem solving
CPM framework 6Nc3, 6Ps5; Teacher's Resource 15.1

2 Complete the diagram for the 4 times table.

The units digit is always even but that does not tell us whether the number is divisible by 4.

Multiples of 4 are:

4, 8, 12, 16, 20

24, 28, 32, 36, 40

44, 48, 52, 56, 60

64, 68, 72, 76, 80

84, 88, 92, 96, 100

Then you can continue counting:

104, 108, 112, 116, 120 and so on

To test whether a number is a multiple of 4, just look at the tens and units only.

Circle the numbers that are divisible by 4.

134   204   154   124   244   214

> **Hint:** You only need to look at the tens and units.

3 **Divisible – a game for two players**

Shuffle the cards 0, 1, 2, 3, 4, 5, 6, 7, 8, 9 and an additional 0 and 5 from resource 1 and lay them out, face down. Take turns to pick four cards at random.

Each player uses the cards to make a four-digit number.

If your number is divisible by 4 score 1 point.
If your number is divisible by 5 score 2 points.
If your number is divisible by 10 score 3 points.
If your number is divisible by 25 score 4 points.

The first player to 10 points is the winner.

Record two of your numbers here:

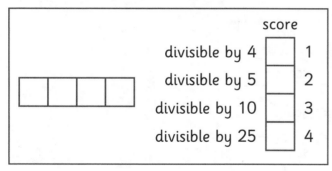

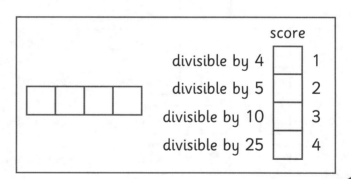

Division

Remember

Division by repeated subtraction

Example:
$204 \div 6 = 34$

```
    2 0 4
  −   6 0   10 × 6
    1 4 4
  −   6 0   10 × 6
      8 4
  −   6 0   10 × 6
      2 4
  −   2 4   4 × 6
        0   34 × 6
```

→

```
    2 0 4
  − 1 8 0   30 × 6
      2 4
  −   2 4   4 × 6
        0   34 × 6
```

Aim to use as few stages as possible.

Fractions and division

$204 \div 6$ could also be written as $\frac{1}{6}$ of 204

To find $\frac{5}{6}$ of 204 divide by 6 to find $\frac{1}{6}$, then multiply by 5 to find $\frac{5}{6}$.

You will need: resource 5, page 85, for activity 3

1 Find the number that can be divided by 7 with a remainder of 1.

74   75   76   84   85   86   94   95   96

2 Remainders – a game for two players

Take turns to use the spinner to generate four digits and use them to make a HTU ÷ U calculation.

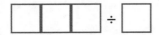

Work out the answer. If there is no remainder, score 3 points.
If the remainder is an even number, score 2 points and if the remainder is an odd number score 1 point. The first player to 10 points is the winner.

 = _____ remainder   score ☐

 = _____ remainder   score ☐

 = _____ remainder   score ☐

 = _____ remainder   score ☐

 = _____ remainder   score ☐

Unit 1A: Number and problem solving, **Unit 2A:** Number and problem solving
CPM framework 6Nc10, 6Nc19, 6Nc20, 6Nc21, 6Pt1, 6Ps1; Teacher's Resource 4.2, 15.3

3   Division can be shown in different ways.

> These expressions are equivalent.
>
> $5\overline{)28}$ $28 \div 5$ $\dfrac{28}{5}$ $\dfrac{1}{5}$ of 28
>
> $28 \div 5 = 5$ remainder 3
>
> The remainder can be expressed as a **fraction**, giving the answer $5\dfrac{3}{5}$, or as a **decimal**, giving the answer 5.6.

Use resource 5 to make sets of three cards:

- a calculation card
- the answer expressed as a mixed number
- the answer expressed as a decimal.

Record your sets here.

4   Use repeated subtraction to work out the division. Write the remainder as a fraction or decimal.

> **Hint:** Try to use as few stages as possible.

$104 \div 5$ $107 \div 4$

$189 \div 2$ $238 \div 4$

5 (a) Find $\dfrac{7}{10}$ of 30   **(b)**   Find $\dfrac{3}{10}$ of 210

Unit 1A: Number and problem solving, **Unit 2A:** Number and problem solving
CPM framework 6Nc10, 6Nc19, 6Nc20, 6Nc21, 6Pt1, 6Ps1; Teacher's Resource 4.2, 15.3

39

Multiplication

Remember

Multiply by halving one number and doubling the other

The answer stays the same so it is possible to work from known facts to derive other facts, for example:

$7 \times 8 = 56$ so $14 \times 4 = 56$

Use number facts to generate other facts

Example: Work out the 17 times table by adding 7 times tables facts to 10 times tables facts.

Multiply HTU by a single digit.

Example: $346 \times 9 = 3114$

Grid method:

	300	40	6
9	2700	360	54

$2700 + 360 + 54 = 3144$

Moving towards a standard method:

```
300 + 40 + 6                      346
         × 9                      × 9
    ─────────                 ─────────
         2700    300 × 9           2700
          360     40 × 9            360
           54      6 × 9             54
    ─────────                 ─────────
         3114                     3114
```

You will need: resource 6, page 86, for activity 1

---

1   Multiplication golf

Use resource 6 to play a game of multiplication golf to practise recalling table facts.

Hint: You can challenge a friend or have a game on your own.

2 Complete the number sentence.

$45 \times 16 = 90 \times \boxed{}$

Use your result to work out 45×16 mentally.

3 Complete the number sentence.

$35 \times 8 = \boxed{} \times 2$

Use your result to work out 35×8 mentally.

Unit 2A: Number and problem solving
CPM framework 6Nc16, 6Nc17, 6Nc18, 6Pt1, 6Ps1; Teacher's Resource 15.2

4 Here are some number facts.

$1 \times 17 = 17$

$2 \times 17 = 34$

$4 \times 17 = 68$

$8 \times 17 = 136$

Use these facts to calculate 13×17.

Show the answer and how you worked it out.

5 Use these facts to work out 68×17. Explain your method.

$70 \times 17 = 1190$ $2 \times 17 = 34$

6 Use the grid method to show that $9 \times 32 = 288$.

Use that fact to work out 27×32.

7 Cross-number puzzle

Complete the cross-number puzzle. Show your working in the space below the clues.

Across

1 171×9
3 8×9
4 528×8
5 502×9
7 253×5
9 732×4
11 224×7
12 128×4
13 157×4
14 774×2
15 6×9

Down

1 361×4
2 158×6
3 927×8
6 748×2
7 3×6
8 628×8
9 513×5
10 956×3
12 117×5

Time

Remember

Time

a.m. stands for *ante meridiem* which is in the morning.
p.m. stands for *post meridiem* which is in the afternoon.
Timetables and many digital watches use the 24-hour clock.
8:00 a.m. is written 08:00
8:00 p.m. is written 20:00

Time intervals

Use a time line to calculate time intervals, for example:
A train departs at 14:10 and arrives at 17:40. How long does the journey take?

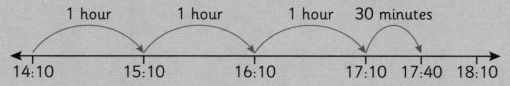

The journey takes 3 hours 30 minutes.

---

1 Use these numbers to complete the sentences.

4   7   12   24   60   100   1000

- There are _____ minutes in an hour.
- There are _____ months in one year.
- There are _____ hours in one day.
- There are _____ years in a century.
- There are _____ days in one week.
- There are _____ years in a millennium.
- There are about _____ weeks in one month.

2 What time does this clock show?
Circle the correct answer.

3:00   3:12   12:03   12:15

3 Which of these times is equivalent to 4 o'clock in the afternoon?
Circle the correct answer.

4 a.m.   04:00   14:00   16:00

4 Orla visits a friend. The clock shows the time as she arrives at her friend's home.

She leaves her friend's home at 8:50 p.m.

How long does she stay at her friend's home? _____

Unit 2B: Measure and problem solving
CPM framework 6Mt1, 6Mt2, 6Mt3, 6Mt5, 6Pt2; Teacher's Resource 18.1

5 Lisa says, 'I arrived at the Sports Club at quarter to eleven and left at 11:25.'

How long did she spend at the Sports Club? _____

6 Here are four times.

A [1 week] B [5 days] C [100 hours] D [600 minutes]

Arrange the times in order of size, starting with the smallest.

Use the letters A, B, C and D. _____

(**Hint:** You will need to do some conversions before you can complete the ordering.)

7 One of these watches is 3 minutes fast. The other watch is 2 minutes slow.

What is the correct time? _____

8 Manjit spent $2\frac{1}{2}$ hours reading on Saturday and 1 hour 20 minutes reading on Sunday.

How long did Manjit spend reading on Saturday and Sunday? _____

9 Four students take part
in a sponsored walk.

The table shows the start
and finish times.

	Start time	Finish time	Time taken
Amira	10:30	11:55	
Bimla	10:35	12:05	
Conrad	10:40	12:08	
Delroy	10:45	12:20	

How long did each student take to complete the walk?

What is the difference in time between the slowest and the fastest walker?

_____

Area and perimeter

Remember

Area of a compound shape

To find the area of a compound shape split the shape into rectangles, for example:

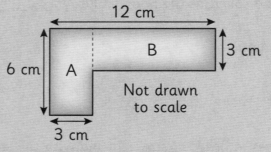

Not drawn to scale

Area of A = 6 × 3 = 18 cm²
Area of B = 9 × 3 = 27 cm²
Total area = 18 + 27 = 45 cm²

There may be alternative ways of splitting up the shape. Sometimes it is more convenient to think of the compound shape fitting inside a rectangle; find the area of the rectangle and subtract the part not required.

Area of an irregular shape

Estimated area = whole squares + squares greater than half shaded.

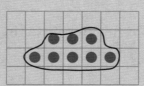

Estimated area = 8 squares

Vocabulary
area,
perimeter

---

1 What is the area of the shaded shape? Give your answer as a number of squares.

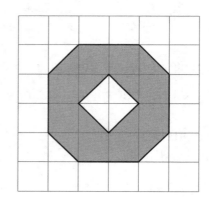

_____

> **Hint:** Count squares and half squares. Give your answer as a number of squares. You may find it helpful to draw the squares on the diagram.

2 Estimate the area of the closed shape.

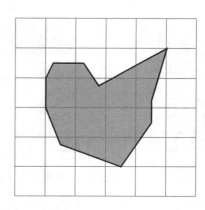

_____

> **Hint:** You may find it helpful to draw the squares on the diagram and use the recording system shown above.

Unit 1B: Measure and problem solving, **Unit 2B:** Measure and problem solving, **Unit 3B:** Measure and problem solving
CPM framework 6Ma1, 6Ma2, 6Ma3; Teacher's Resource 7.1, 19.1, 32.1, 32.2

3 Here are four shapes on a grid.

Which two shapes have the same **area**? _____

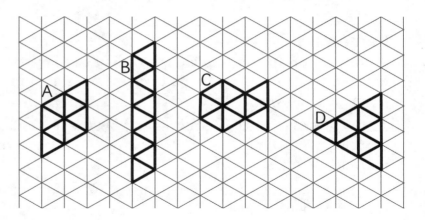

4 Complete this table of information about a rectangle.

Length (cm)	Width (cm)	Area (cm²)	Perimeter (cm)
	2 cm		16 cm

Hint: You will need to find the length first.

5 Here is a rectangle.

It is twice as long as it is wide.

What is the perimeter of the rectangle? _____

What is the area of the rectangle? _____

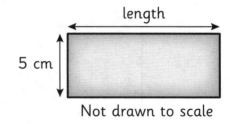

Not drawn to scale

6 Find the area of each shape. Show your working.

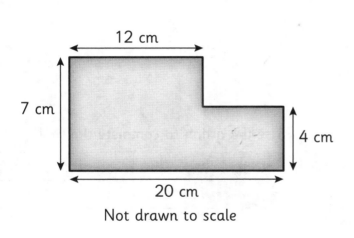

Not drawn to scale

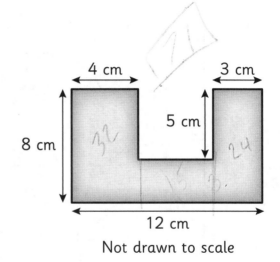

Not drawn to scale

Unit 1B: Measure and problem solving, **Unit 2B:** Measure and problem solving, **Unit 3B:** Measure and problem solving
CPM framework 6Ma1, 6Ma2, 6Ma3; Teacher's Resource 7.1, 19.1, 32.1, 32.2

45

Using data

Vocabulary

conversion graph

1   Here is a conversion graph for miles and kilometres.

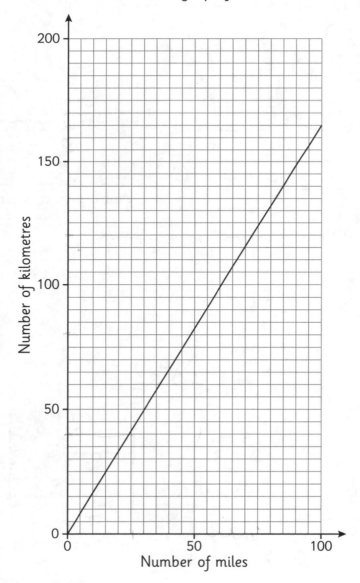

Use the graph to complete the table.

miles	25			100
kilometres		80	120	

Unit 2C: Handling data and problem solving
CPM framework 6Dh1, 6Ps2; Teacher's Resource 20.1

2   Here is a conversion graph for dollars and pounds.

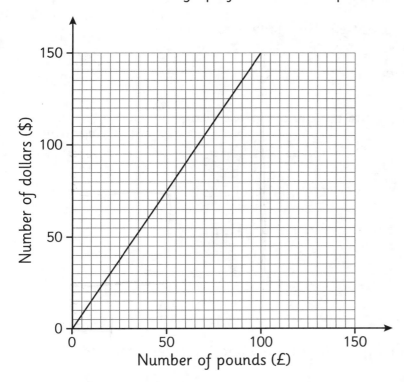

Marie changes £100 to dollars at the beginning of a holiday.
How many dollars does she get? _____

When she returns Marie changes $25 back into pounds.
How many pounds does she get? _____

3   The graph shows the ages of players at a football club.

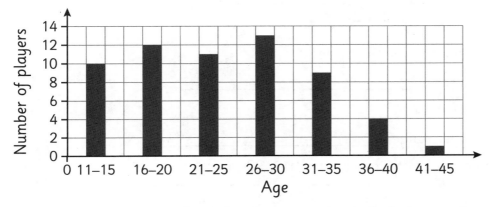

How many players belong to the club? _____

How many players are 25 or younger? _____

A player aged 32 joins the club.

Add this information to the graph.

Mode and range

Remember

The **mode** is the data item that occurs most often. The mode is one type of average.

The **difference** between the highest number and the lowest number is called the **range**.

The word **range** is used in phrases such as **age range** and **price range**.

Example

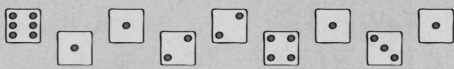

The mode is 1 and the range is 5.
The range is the difference between 6, the highest number and 1, the lowest number.

You will need:
resource 7, page 87, for activity 2

Vocabulary
mode, range

1   The Leisure Centre

The youngest member of a Leisure Centre is 15 years old and the oldest member is 81 years old.

What is the age range? _____

The table shows the different attendances for the swimming class for two weeks.

Week 1	Attendance
Monday	26
Wednesday	16
Thursday	25
Total	

Week 2	Attendance
Monday	51
Wednesday	33
Thursday	18
Total	

Complete the total attendance for each week.

What is the range for week 1? _____

What is the range for week 2? _____

Which week has the bigger range? _____

The table shows the time taken by five boys to run 200 metres.

Name	Khalid	Leroy	Chen	Erik	Lucas
Time	35 secs	29 secs	32 secs	34 secs	32 secs

What is the range of times? _____

What is the mode? _____

Unit 2C: Handling data and problem solving
CPM framework 6Dh3, 6Ps4; Teacher's Resource 21.1

2 Cut out the 12 jigsaw pieces of the mode and range jigsaw found on page 87.

Reassemble by matching each data set to the correct mode and range.

Stick down your pieces.

Mean and median

Remember

There are three types of average: mean, median and mode.

Example: Find the mean and the median of 13, 6, 6, 8, 7.

The **median** is the middle number when the numbers are arranged in order of size.
- Put the numbers in order of size: 6, 6, 7, 8, 13.
- The median is 7.

The **mean** is the total divided by the number of items.
- Add the numbers: 13 + 6 + 6 + 8 + 7 = 40.
- Divide by 5: 40 ÷ 5 = 8.
- The mean is 8.

Vocabulary

average, mean, median

1   The table shows the time taken by five boys to run 200 metres.

Name	Khalid	Leroy	Chen	Erik	Lucas
Time (seconds)	35	29	32	34	32

What is the median time? _____

> **Hint:** Arrange the times in order of size, then decide which is the middle one in the list.

2   Here is a set of numbers. Add a number to the list to make 7 the median.

4, 11, 8, 7, 5, 3, ☐   median 7

> **Hint:** You need to make 7 the middle number when the numbers are in order of size.

3   The table shows the distance, in kilometres, that Leena cycled on 5 days.

Day	1	2	3	4	5
Distance (km)	22	47	26	33	47

Find the **mean** number of kilometres that Leena cycled each day.

> Mean distance travelled = total distance ÷ number of days
>
> Total distance =
>
> Mean distance =

Unit 2C: Handling data and problem solving
CPM framework 6Dh3, 6Ps4; Teacher's Resource 21.1

4 Here are ten number cards. Each card represents the number of merits awarded to ten students during a week.

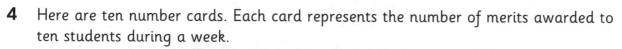

Find the mean number of merits awarded.

5 Here are nine dominoes.

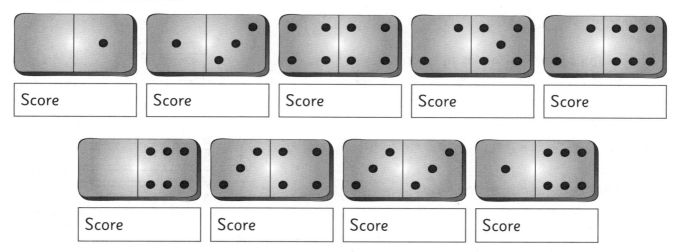

Score	Score	Score	Score	Score

Score	Score	Score	Score

Count the total number of spots on each domino and record the score

What is the median score? _____

What is the mean score? _____

6 Here are five product cards.

Product	Product	Product	Product	Product

Find the product of the two numbers on each card. Record the results.

What is the median product? _____

What is the mean product? _____

What is the mode of the products? _____

Statistics in everyday life

Remember

Statistics are used to analyse what is happening in the world around us. They tell us what happened in the past and can be useful in predicting what may happen in the future, for example:

- weather forecasters use statistics to help predict the weather
- shops use statistics to plan the ordering of goods
- companies use statistics to help with quality control.

Sometimes statistics are presented in a confusing way to grab our attention.

1 Fatima places ten boxes of shoes on a shelf.
Each box shows the size of the shoes packed in it.

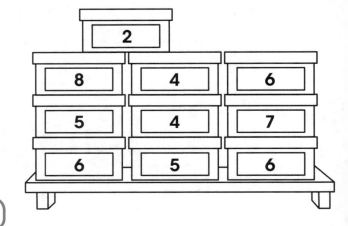

What is the mode of the sizes? _____
What is the range of sizes? _____

> **Hint:** You may need to look back at page 48.

2 Here are two graphs showing the attendance in Class 5 during one week.

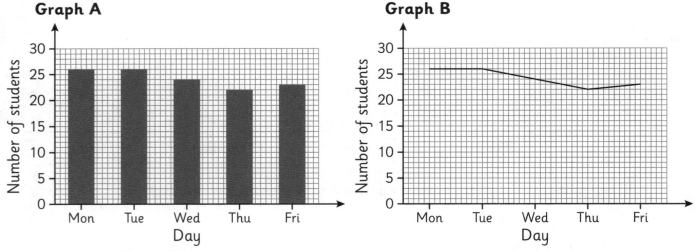

Karim says, Graph B is not an appropriate way to show this information.

His teacher agrees with him. Explain why Karim is correct.

3 There are three people in Mei's family.

The range of shoe sizes is 4.

Two people in the family wear shoe size 6.

Mei's shoe size is not 6 and not 10.

What is Mei's shoe size? _____

4 The bar charts show how many students went to an after-school club.

> **Hint:** The zigzag mark on the vertical axis is used when the scale does not start at zero.

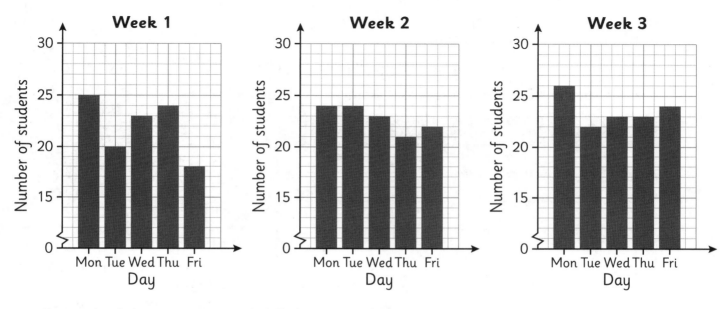

For each of the statements tick (✓) the correct box and give a reason for your answer.

Helga says, 'The same number of students went to the club each Wednesday'.

True ☐   False ☐   Insufficient information ☐

Explain how you know.

Vincent says, 'The same students went to the club each Wednesday.'

True ☐   False ☐   Insufficient information ☐

Explain how you know.

Probability

Remember

Probability is a measure of how likely something is to happen. The probability of an event may not match the actual outcome, for example, the probability of a coin landing on heads or tails is equally likely but you may throw heads 3 times in a row.

Probabilities can be represented on a **probability scale**.

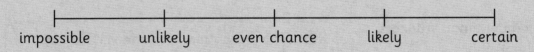

impossible   unlikely   even chance   likely   certain

Vocabulary
probability, certain, likely, unlikely, impossible, even chance

1   This spinner is a regular hexagon.

     The numbers 1, 2, 3, 4, 5 and 6 are equally likely to come up.

     Use the spinner 40 times and record the outcomes in the table.

Outcome	Tally	Frequency
1		
2		
3		
4		
5		
6		

Write a sentence to explain your results.

Hint: Remember the actual results may be different to those you expect.
The **outcome** is what happens.

2   When you toss a coin you can get a head or a tail.

     Toss a coin 40 times and record the outcomes in the table.

Outcome	Tally	Frequency
Head		
Tail		

Write a sentence to explain your results.

Hint: Try combining your outcomes with those of your friends to give a larger frequency. You may find this result is closer to your expectations.

Unit 3A: Number and problem solving
CPM framework 6Db1; Teacher's Resource 22.1

3 This spinner is a **regular hexagon**.

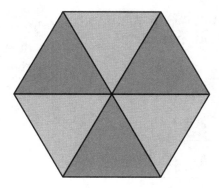

Write a whole number in each section of the spinner so that:

- it is **certain** you will get a number less than 5

- it is **impossible** you will get an odd number.

5 This spinner is a **regular octagon**.

Which two different numbers are equally likely to come up? _____

Explain why 3 has an even chance of coming up.

> **Hint:** For the explanation you will need to compare outcomes of 1 and 2 against 3.

6 Yuri uses a spinner shaped as a regular octagon.

What is the probability that he spins:

a number less than 10 _____

the number 10 _____

an even number? _____

4 This spinner is a **regular octagon**.

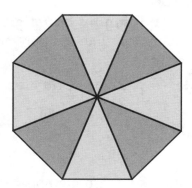

Write 1, 2 or 3 in each section of the spinner so that:

- 1 and 3 are equally likely to come up

- 2 is most likely to come up.

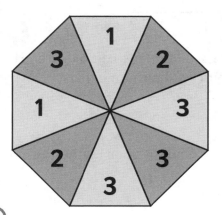

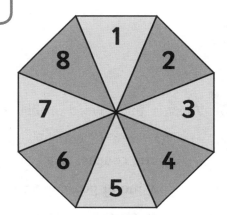

> **Hint:** Use the words in the vocabulary section to answer this question.
> A similar question could be used in stage 5 where you **are given a list of options** to choose from. By stage 6, you are expected to know the vocabulary and choose your own words.

Multiplication

Remember

When **multiplying by two-digit numbers**, you can continue to use the grid method or you may prefer to use a standard method, provided you understand the method.

You will need: the spinner or a dice for activity 3

Example: 56×27 Grid method:

×	50	6	
20	1000	120	1120
7	350	42	392
			1512

Developing a standard method:

```
    50 + 6                56
  × 20 + 7              × 27
     1000   50 × 20     1120   56 × 20
      120    6 × 20      392   56 × 7
      350   50 × 7      1512
       42    6 × 7
     1512
```

These methods can be extended to multiply three- and four-digit numbers by two-digit numbers.

1 Choose your method to answer these.

78×34 67×43 61×97 34×46

2 Answer these word problems.

- There are 13 coaches on an excursion. Each coach seats 52 passengers. All the coaches are full.

  How many passengers are there altogether?

- A train ticket costs $78. What would be the total cost of four tickets?

Hint: Set down your work clearly and answer the question using the correct units. The first one is a number of passengers.

Unit 2A: Number and problem solving, **Unit 3A:** Number and problem solving
CPM framework 6Nc18, 6Pt1, 6Ps1, 6Ps6; Teacher's Resource 15.2, 24.2

3 Dice multiplication – a game for two players

Player 1 rolls the dice or spins the spinner twice to make a
two-digit number and writes it in the appropriate space, then
repeats to form the second two-digit number. Player 2 does
the same. Both players multiply their two numbers together
and write the answers in the answer box. The winner of the
round is the player with the **larger** answer. The overall
winner is the player who wins the most rounds.

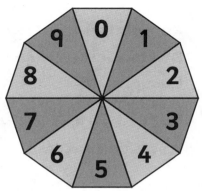

Example round:

	Player 1	Player 2	Winner	Working out
two-digit number	63	74		
two-digit number	41	52	Player 2	
Answer	2583	3848		

	Player 1	Player 2	Winner	Working out
two-digit number				
two-digit number				
Answer				

	Player 1	Player 2	Winner	Working out
two-digit number				
two-digit number				
Answer				

	Player 1	Player 2	Winner	Working out
two-digit number				
two-digit number				
Answer				

	Player 1	Player 2	Winner	Working out
two-digit number				
two-digit number				
Answer				

Unit 2A: Number and problem solving, **Unit 3A:** Number and problem solving
CPM framework 6Nc18, 6Pt1, 6Ps1, 6Ps6; Teacher's Resource 15.2, 24.2

57

Division

Remember

Dividing a three-digit number by a two-digit number

Example: $552 \div 24$

Start by multiplying 24 by multiples of 10 to get an estimate.

As $24 \times 20 = 480$ and $24 \times 30 = 720$, the answer lies between 20 and 30

Repeated subtraction

$$
\begin{array}{r}
24\overline{)552} \\
-480 \quad 24 \times 20 \\
\hline
72 \\
-72 \quad 24 \times 3 \\
\hline
0 \quad 24 \times 23
\end{array}
$$

Answer 23

The final stage is to move to the long division algorithm where the digits of the answer are recorded above the line as shown below:

$$
\begin{array}{r}
23 \\
24\overline{)552} \\
-480 \\
\hline
72 \\
-72 \\
\hline
0
\end{array}
$$

Answer 23

1 Choose your method to answer these.

$546 \div 26$ $\qquad$ $476 \div 34$ $\qquad$ $893 \div 47$ $\qquad$ $874 \div 23$

2 Making a jigsaw

On page 49, you assembled a jigsaw. In this unit, you are going to follow the instructions to make a division jigsaw.

- Use the space around the jigsaw grid to work out the answers to each calculation written on the jigsaw pieces. Continue on a separate sheet of paper if necessary.
- Add the answers to the boxes on the jigsaw. All answers are whole numbers.
- Make a copy. Cut out the pieces and give it to a friend to complete.

Unit 2A: Number and problem solving, **Unit 3A:** Number and problem solving
CPM framework 6Nc19, 6Pt1, 6Ps1; Teacher's Resource 15.3, 24.2

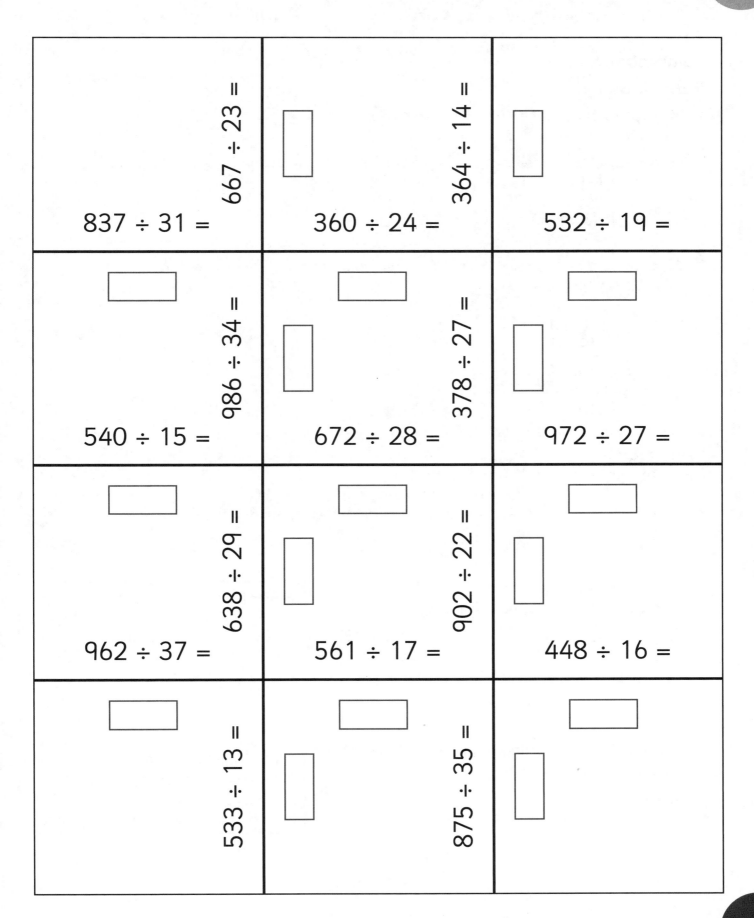

$837 \div 31 =$

$667 \div 23 =$

$360 \div 24 =$

$364 \div 14 =$

$532 \div 19 =$

$540 \div 15 =$

$986 \div 34 =$

$672 \div 28 =$

$378 \div 27 =$

$972 \div 27 =$

$962 \div 37 =$

$638 \div 29 =$

$561 \div 17 =$

$902 \div 22 =$

$448 \div 16 =$

$533 \div 13 =$

$875 \div 35 =$

Unit 2A: Number and problem solving, **Unit 3A:** Number and problem solving
CPM framework 6Nc19, 6Pt1, 6Ps1; Teacher's Resource 15.3, 24.2

59

The laws of arithmetic

Remember

Multiplication rules

1 Multiplication can be done in any order for example:
$65 \times 78 = 78 \times 65$

2 Finding factors of one number can make it easier to multiply, for example:
$$8.1 \times 60 = 8.1 \times (10 \times 6)$$
$$= (8.1 \times 6) \times 10$$
$$= 48.6 \times 10$$
$$= 486$$

3 Partitioning one number, multiplying the two parts and recombining, for example:
$$17 \times 32 = 17 \times (30 + 2)$$
$$= (17 \times 30) + (17 \times 2)$$
$$= 510 + 34$$
$$= 544$$

$$17 \times 29 = 17 \times (30 - 1)$$
$$= (17 \times 30) - (17 \times 1)$$
$$= 510 - 17$$
$$= 493$$

Using brackets

Calculate whatever is inside the brackets first.
$(3 \times 4) + 3 = 15$ (Calculate 3×4, then add on 3)
$3 \times (7 + 3) = 30$ (Work out $7 + 3$ in the bracket, then multiply by 3)

---

1 Complete these calculations.
Show all the stages of your working.

$5 \times (70 + 1)$ $6 \times (60 - 3)$

> **Hint:** Use rule 3 above to help you.
> Example 1 becomes $(5 \times 70) + (5 \times 1)$
> Now continue the calculation.

2 Use brackets and partitioning to work these out.
Show all your working.

3×67 8×93

> **Hint:** Example 1 becomes
> $3 \times (60 + 7) = (3 \times 60) + (3 \times 7)$
> or $3 \times (70 - 3) = (3 \times 70) - (3 \times 3)$
> Now continue one of the calculations.

Unit 3A: Number and problem solving
CPM framework 6Nc22, 6Ps6; Teacher's Resource 26.1

3 Complete these calculations.
Show all the stages of your working.

4.3 × 50

6.1 × 40

> **Hint:** Use rule 2 above to help you
> Example 1 becomes 4.3 × (10 × 5)
> Now continue the calculation.

4 Put one set of brackets in each calculation to make them correct.

3 × 8 + 2 = 30

9 − 4 × 2 = 10

> **Hint:** Remember brackets are used as an instruction to do this part of the calculation first. Without them the convention is to do multiplication and division before addition and subtraction.

5 Work out the answer to each calculation.

Join each calculation to the correct answer.

The first one has been done for you.

(12 − 3) × 8	18
10 × 8 + 1	27
6 × (5 − 2)	36
7 × (4 + 5)	45
6 × (3 + 6)	54
(9 − 4) × 9	63
(8 + 4) × 3	72
(12 − 3) × 3	81

6 Write the missing numbers to make these calculations correct.

10 × (☐ − 10) = 10

(10 − ☐) × 10 = 10

> **Hint:** Work out what the calculation in the bracket must be.

Fractions

Remember

Equivalent fractions are equal in value, for example

$$\underset{\times 2}{\overset{\times 2}{\frac{3}{5} = \frac{6}{10}}} \qquad \underset{\div 3}{\overset{\div 3}{\frac{12}{15} = \frac{4}{5}}}$$

You normally write the fraction with the smallest possible denominator, referred to as the **simplest form**.

You may be asked to simplify a fraction (cancel), for example $\frac{8}{10}$ simplifies to $\frac{4}{5}$.

Vocabulary

numerator, denominator, equivalent, simplest form, cancel

1 This fraction wall shows halves, quarters and eighths.

Use the wall to help you complete these questions.

$$\frac{1}{4} = \frac{}{8} \qquad \frac{1}{2} = \frac{}{8} \qquad \frac{3}{4} = \frac{}{8}$$

Which is larger $\frac{5}{8}$ or $\frac{3}{4}$?

You can compare fractions only when they have the same denominator or by looking at them on a number line.

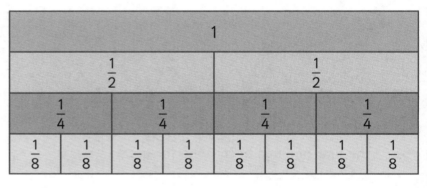

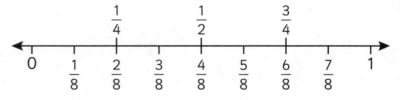

2 Here is a number line marked in tenths.

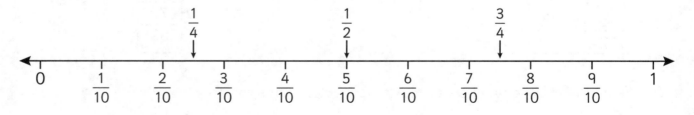

Simplify $\frac{2}{10}, \frac{4}{10}, \frac{6}{10}$ and $\frac{8}{10}$ then add your answers to the number line.

Unit 3A: Number and problem solving
CPM framework 6Nn21, 6Nn22, 6Nn26; Teacher's Resource 27.1

3 Equivalent fractions – a game for two players

Players take turns to spin the spinner. The player must choose a fraction from their part of the record sheet, which when written in the simplest form has a denominator the same as the number on the spinner. The player writes the simplified fraction in the box, for example:

Player 1 spins a 5 and writes $\frac{2}{5}$ in the box against the fraction $\frac{6}{15}$.

The winner is the first player to complete all their boxes.

Player 1

$\frac{20}{25} =$ ☐ $\frac{2}{6} =$ ☐ $\frac{2}{12} =$ ☐ $\frac{9}{12} =$ ☐ $\frac{5}{10} =$ ☐ $\frac{2}{8} =$ ☐

$\frac{15}{18} =$ ☐ $\frac{2}{10} =$ ☐ $\frac{6}{15} =$ ☐ $\frac{12}{20} =$ ☐ $\frac{2}{4} =$ ☐ $\frac{6}{9} =$ ☐

Player 2

$\frac{15}{25} =$ ☐ $\frac{4}{6} =$ ☐ $\frac{10}{12} =$ ☐ $\frac{3}{12} =$ ☐ $\frac{4}{10} =$ ☐ $\frac{6}{8} =$ ☐

$\frac{3}{18} =$ ☐ $\frac{3}{6} =$ ☐ $\frac{3}{15} =$ ☐ $\frac{16}{20} =$ ☐ $\frac{4}{8} =$ ☐ $\frac{3}{9} =$ ☐

4 Write $\frac{24}{32}$ in its simplest form.

> **Hint:** Divide the numerator and the denominator by the same number. Make sure you can not simplify the fraction any further.

5 Which is larger $\frac{4}{5}$ or $\frac{7}{10}$?
Explain your answer.

> **Hint:** Find equivalent fractions with the same denominator.

Mixed numbers and improper fractions

Remember

$1\frac{2}{3}$ is called a **mixed number** because it is made up of a whole number and a fraction.

$\frac{5}{3}$ is the equivalent **improper fraction**, because the numerator is larger than the denominator.

Changing an improper fraction to a mixed number

Example: $\frac{17}{5}$

Find out how many whole numbers there are by division: $17 \div 5 = 3$ remainder 2

That is 3 whole ones and two-fifths written as $3\frac{2}{5}$

Changing a mixed number to an improper fraction

Example: $2\frac{1}{8}$

Change 2 whole ones to eighths by multiplying $2 \times 8 = 16$

Add on the 1 eighth

That is 17 eighths written as $\frac{17}{8}$

You will need: resource 8, page 88 for activity 4

Vocabulary
numerator,
denominator,
mixed number,
improper fraction

---

1 Convert these improper fractions to mixed numbers.

$\frac{18}{5} =$ $\frac{15}{8} =$

$\frac{23}{4} =$ $\frac{16}{5} =$

2 Convert these mixed numbers to improper fractions.

$4\frac{3}{8} =$ $8\frac{1}{3} =$

$5\frac{3}{4} =$ $6\frac{2}{3} =$

3 Draw an arrow on the number line to show the position of $1\frac{3}{4}$.

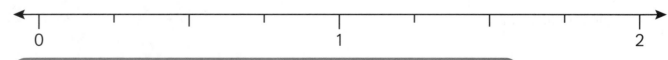

> **Hint:** To work out the denominator of the fraction count the spaces between two consecutive whole numbers.

Unit 3A: Number and problem solving
CPM framework 6Nn24, 6Nn25; Teacher's Resource 27.2

4 Fraction pairs – a game for two players

Cut out the 16 playing cards from the resource.

Shuffle the cards and spread them face down. Take turns to pick two cards.
If they are equivalent, keep the pair. If not, put them back.

Keep going until there are no cards left. The player with the most cards wins.

Record the pairs of equivalent mixed numbers and improper fractions.

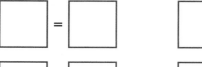 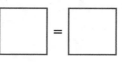 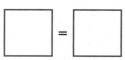

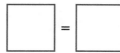 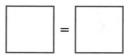 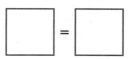

> **Hint:** This game gives practice in converting mixed numbers and improper fractions. Keep the cards safe and practise pairing them up regularly.

5 Here is part of a number line. Write in the two missing mixed numbers.

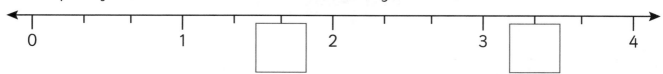

6 Write a mixed number that is greater than $\frac{8}{4}$ and less than $\frac{12}{4}$.

> **Hint:** There are many different possible answers.
> You could choose an improper fraction, then change it to a mixed number.

7 How many thirds are there in $2\frac{2}{3}$?

> **Hint:** This is a different way of asking you to convert a mixed number to an improper fraction. The answer is the numerator of the improper fraction.

8 Here is part of a number line.

Write in the two missing mixed numbers.

Fractions and decimals

Remember

$\frac{1}{2} = 0.5$ $\frac{1}{4} = 0.25$ $\frac{1}{5} = 0.2$ $\frac{1}{10} = 0.1$

$\frac{1}{3} = 0.\dot{3}$ $\frac{2}{3} = 0.\dot{6}$

$\frac{1}{3}$ and $\frac{2}{3}$ are recurring – they go on and on.

To **convert a fraction to a decimal** divide the numerator by the denominator, for example:

$\frac{3}{5} = 3 \div 5 = 0.6$

You will need: different coloured pens for activity 2, resource 9, page 89 for activity 3

Vocabulary
proper fraction

1 Join each fraction to the equivalent decimal.
One has been done for you.

| 0.2 | 0.75 | 0.6 | 0.4 | 0.5 | 0.25 | 0.01 | 0.3 |

| $\frac{1}{2}$ | $\frac{1}{5}$ | $\frac{1}{4}$ | $\frac{1}{100}$ | $\frac{2}{5}$ | $\frac{3}{10}$ | $\frac{3}{4}$ | $\frac{3}{5}$ |

2 Decimal and fraction equivalents – a game for two players

Each choose a different coloured pen.

Take turns to choose two numbers from the circle and arrange them to make a proper fraction.

Convert the fraction to a decimal.

Find the answer on the board and write down your fraction in the box.

Some decimals can be made in more than one way.

When all the boxes contain at least one answer play stops and the winner is the player who has written the most fractions.

0.5	0.01	0.4	0.2
0.1	0.04	0.02	
0.05	0.25		
0.8	0.08		

Circle numbers: 1   2   4   5   8   10   100

Unit 3A: Number and problem solving
CPM framework 6Nn23, 6Nn27; Teacher's Resource 28.1

3 Matching cards – an activity for two players

Cut up the cards from resource 9 and place them in a pile, face down.

Take it in turns to pick a small card and see if it matches any of the numbers on the grid. If your partner agrees with your decision, place the small card next to the appropriate number, or in a discard pile if it does not match.

0.5	0.01	0.4
0.2	0.3	0.1

Make a list of the cards that you discarded. Convert each fraction to a decimal. One has been done for you.

discarded card   decimal

| one third | = | 0.3̇ |

| | = | |

discarded card   decimal

| | = | |

| | = | |

4 Circle three numbers that total 1.

0.3 $\dfrac{1}{2}$ $\dfrac{3}{4}$ 0.1 0.40 0.25

> **Hint:** Change the fractions to decimals before attempting to add the numbers.

5 Circle all the fractions that are not equivalent to 0.5.

$\dfrac{1}{2}$ $\dfrac{2}{4}$ $\dfrac{3}{5}$ $\dfrac{5}{10}$ $\dfrac{5}{100}$

> **Hint:** You will need to change the fractions to decimals.

Percentages

Remember

Per cent means 'out of 100'

50% is $\frac{50}{100} = \frac{1}{2}$ 25% is $\frac{25}{100} = \frac{1}{4}$ 10% is $\frac{10}{100} = \frac{1}{10}$ 1% is $\frac{1}{100}$

Finding a percentage of a quantity

Example: Find 10% of 760

$10\% = \frac{1}{10}$

$760 \div 10 = 76$

If you know 1% of a quantity and 10% of the same quantity, you can work out other percentages.

Example: Find 13% of 760

1% of 760 = 7.6 and 10% of 760 = 76

13% of 760 = 76 + 7.6 + 7.6 + 7.6 = 98.8

---

1   Draw a line to join each fraction to a percentage of the same value.   Fraction $\boxed{\frac{1}{4}}$ $\boxed{\frac{1}{5}}$ $\boxed{\frac{1}{10}}$ $\boxed{\frac{1}{2}}$

Percentage $\boxed{50\%}$ $\boxed{4\%}$ $\boxed{20\%}$ $\boxed{25\%}$ $\boxed{10\%}$

2   The grid has 20 squares. What percentage of the grid is shaded?

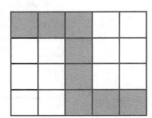

_____

3   Use the number lines to record percentages of quantities.

Find 10% of the quantity, then use your answer to find 20%, 30% and so on. Write the answers under the percentages.

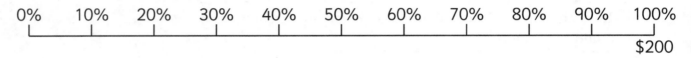

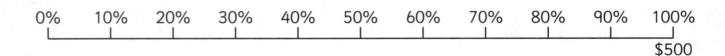

Unit 3A: Number and problem solving
CPM framework 6Nn28, 6Nn29, 6Ps8; Teacher's Resource 28.2

4 First to 100 – a game for 2–4 players

Take turns to spin the spinner.

Decide whether to find 1% or 10% of the number.

Work out the answer and keep a running total of your scores.

For example, if the scores of the first three rounds are 60, 20 and 4 the recording sheet will look like this.

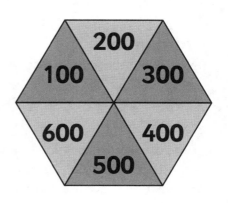

Number	1% or 10%	Answer	Running total
600	10%	60	60
200	10%	20	80
400	1%	4	84

Hint: A **running total** is the sum of the numbers recorded so far.

Play continues until one player reaches 100 without 'going over'. A player may stop at any time and keep their final score but if a player 'goes over' 100 they are out. Other players continue playing, aiming to get as close to 100 as possible. The winner is the player who is closest to 100.

Recording sheets

Number	1% or 10%	Answer	Running total

Number	1% or 10%	Answer	Running total

Ratio and proportion

Remember

Ratio compares **part to part**.

For every grey circle, there are 4 white circles.

A **proportion** compares **part to whole**. It can be given as a fraction, as a decimal or as a percentage. 'What proportion?' means 'What fraction?', or 'What decimal?', or 'What percentage?'

Example

There are 10 circles altogether.

1 out of 5 circles is grey ($\frac{1}{5}$, 0.2, 20%)

4 out of 5 circles are white ($\frac{4}{5}$, 0.8, 80%)

You will need: resource 10, page 90, for activity 5

Vocabulary

ratio, proportion

Questions rarely use the words ratio or proportion. Instead they use the language found in the Remember section.

1 Two pencils have the same length as five protractors.

How many protractors would have the same length as 10 pencils? _____

> **Hint:** Find out how many lots of 2 there are in 10 (pencils). That will tell you how many lots of 5 (protractors) you need.

2 Heidi arranges flowers in a vase.

She uses 3 red flowers **for every** 4 white flowers.

She uses 12 red flowers.

How many white flowers does she use? _____

> **Hint:** See **for every** in the ratio section above.

Unit 3A: Number and problem solving
CPM framework 6Nn30, 6Ps7; Teacher's Resource 29.1

3 Pierre makes a fruit salad using melon, mango and kiwi fruit.

For every melon he uses 2 mangoes and 5 kiwi fruits.

He uses 16 fruits altogether.

How many kiwi fruits does he use?

4 Ali is cooking pasta.

The recipe says he needs 300 grams for 4 people.

How much pasta does he need for 12 people?

5 You will need to work with a partner for this activity.

Cut out the twelve ratio and proportion cards from resource 10.

- Work in pairs to draw a set of shapes to match the information on each card, for example:

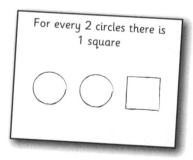

For every 2 circles there is 1 square

- Arrange the cards into four groups. Each group should have the same set of shapes, that are described in different ways.

- Draw a set of matching cards.

Metric and imperial measures

Remember

The **imperial system** of measurement is an old measurement system based on everyday activities that originated in England. Most countries now use the **metric system** of measurement but imperial units remain in everyday use.

13 feet is approximately equal to 3.8 metres

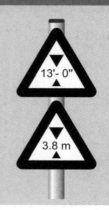

Vocabulary

imperial, metric

1 Magda weighs 650 grams of beans.

Draw an arrow (↓) on the scale to show 650 grams.

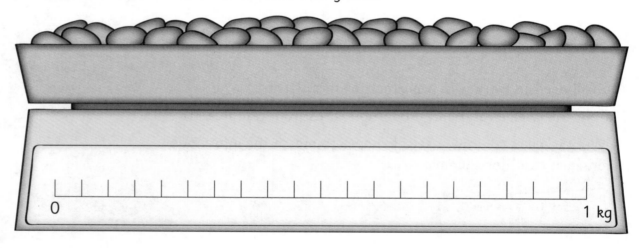

2 Complete the grids showing conversions of metric measures:

Kilograms and grams

1 kg	0.5 kg		1 g	0.75 kg	0.7 kg
1000 g		100 g			

Metres, centimetres and millimetres

1 m	0.001 m	0.5 m			
100 cm			75 cm		25 cm
1000 mm	1 mm			400 mm	

> **Hint:** Use the entries in the first column of each table to help you with the conversions.

3 Use these approximate conversions to answer the question.

Metric	Imperial
1 litre	1.8 pints
1 kilogram	2.2 pounds
8 kilometres	5 miles
2.5 centimetres	1 inch

Here are four pairs of measurements.

Draw a ring around the smaller measurement in each pair.

The first one has been done for you.

3 miles	(3 kilometres)
4 pints	4 litres
5 pounds	5 grams
6 inches	6 centimetres

4 A petrol station shows this information.
How many gallons is 40 litres?

10 LITRES = 2.2 GALLONS

5 A cookery book shows this conversion table.

Mass in ounces	Mass in grams
1	25
2	50
3	75
4	110
5	150
10	270

Use the table to explain how you can tell the conversions **cannot be exact**.

> **Hint:** It is important to remember that **all conversions are approximate**.

Unit 2B: Measure and problem solving, **Unit 3B:** Measure and problem solving
CPM framework 6MI1, 6MI2, 6MI3, 6MI5, 6Pt2; Teacher's Resource 17.1, 17.2, 30.1, 30.2

73

Time zones, timetables and calendars

Remember

Time zones

The world is divided into time zones using negative and positive offsets starting from the Greenwich Meridian.

Vocabulary

offset, meridian

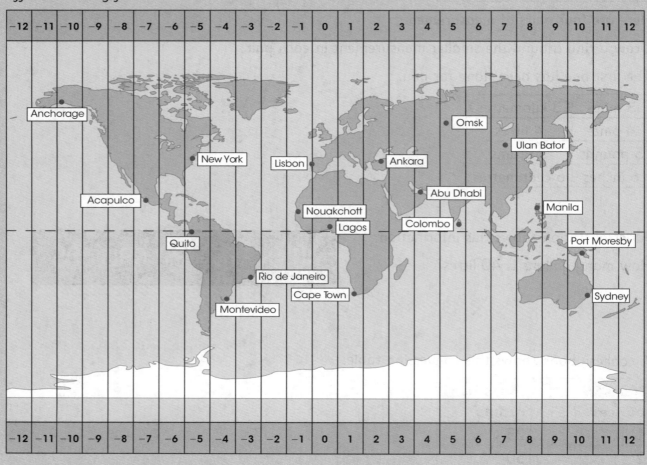

It is 11:15 in London.

At the same time, it is 08:15 in Rio de Janeiro, 15:15 in Abu Dhabi and 18:15 in Ulan Bator.

London

Buenos Aires

Dubai

Beijing

Unit 1B: Measure and problem solving, Unit 2B: Measure and problem solving, Unit 3B: Measure and problem solving
CPM framework 6Mt4, 6Mt6, 6Mt7, 6Mt8, 6Pt2; Teacher's Resource 6.1, 6.2, 18.2, 31.1, 31.2

1   It is 5 July.

Tara is counting the days to her birthday on 7 August.

How many days does she count?

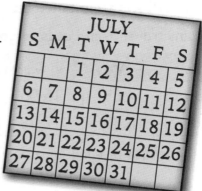

2   What is the date of the third Tuesday in December?

3   Buses leave Oaktown every 15 minutes.

Write the missing time.

Depart Oaktown	08:25	08:40	08:55	

Trains leave Oaktown every 20 minutes

Write the missing time.

Depart Oaktown		11:25	11:45	12:00

4   Rio de Janeiro is 5 hours behind the time in Athens.

- It is 1 pm in Athens.

  What time is it in Rio de Janeiro?

  _____

- It is 10 am in Rio de Janeiro.

  What time is it in Athens?

  _____

Unit 1B: Measure and problem solving, Unit 2B: Measure and problem solving, Unit 3B: Measure and problem solving
CPM framework 6Mt4, 6Mt6, 6Mt7, 6Mt8, 6Pt2; Teacher's Resource 6.1, 6.2, 18.2, 31.1, 31.2

75

5 Here is part of a train timetable.

Six trains travel from Leeds to London.

Train	A	B	C	D	E	F
Leeds	14:05	15:05	16:16	16:45	17:16	17:45
London	16:40	17:48	18:46	19:21	19:53	20:30

Find the length of each journey in hours and minutes.

Calculate the number of **minutes** taken by Train F. _____

Which trains take less than 2 hours 40 minutes to travel from Leeds to London?

Write the letters. _____

> **Hint:** Draw a time line to work out a time interval.

6 It is 12 noon in London. These clocks show the time in other cities.

| Buenos Aires | London | Dubai | Beijing |

When it is 15:30 in London what time is it in Buenos Airies? _____

When it is 5 p.m. in Dubai what time is it in Beijing? _____

When it is midnight in Beijing what time is it in London? _____

Unit 1B: Measure and problem solving, **Unit 2B:** Measure and problem solving, **Unit 3B:** Measure and problem solving
CPM framework 6Mt4, 6Mt5, 6Mt6, 6Mt7, 6Mt8, 6Pt2; Teacher's Resource 6.1, 6.2, 18.2, 31.1, 31.2

2D shapes

Remember

Polygons are straight-sided closed shapes. The polygon is **regular** if all the sides are of equal length and all the angles are the same size.

Vocabulary

polygon, quadrilateral, rhombus, parallelogram, trapezium, kite

Quadrilaterals

Square: 4 equal sides, 4 right angles
Rectangle: 2 pairs of equal sides, 4 right angles
Rhombus: 4 equal sides, opposite sides equal and parallel
Parallelogram: Opposite sides equal and parallel
Trapezium: One pair of parallel sides of different lengths
Kite: Adjacent sides equal, one pair of opposite angles equal

1 Match each quadrilateral to the correct description.
One has been done for you.

Description **Quadrilateral**

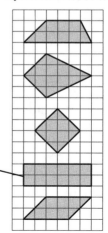

| Opposite sides are equal and parallel |
| Only one pair of parallel sides |
| Four equal angles, opposite sides are equal and parallel |
| All sides are equal, all angles are right angles |
| Adjacent sides are equal, one pair of opposite angles are equal |

2 Here is a shape on a grid.

For each statement put a tick (✓) if it is true.
Put a cross (✗) if it is not true.

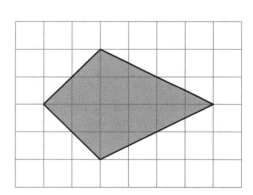

☐ The shape is a quadrilateral.

☐ The shape is a parallelogram.

☐ The shape has 1 right angle.

☐ The shape has 2 lines of symmetry.

Unit 1C: Geometry and problem solving, **Unit 3C:** Geometry and problem solving
CPM framework 6Gs1, 6Gs3, 6Pt4; Teacher's Resource 8.1, 34.1

77

3 Here are the names of five quadrilaterals.

kite   square   parallelogram   rectangle   rhombus

Write the name of each shape in the sorting diagram.

One has been done for you.

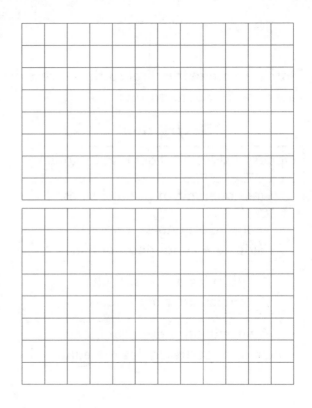

> **Hint:** A shape has rotational symmetry if, when it is turned around its centre point, it matches the original outline more than once. An equilateral triangle has rotational symmetry order 3.

Has no symmetry	Has reflective symmetry only	Has rotational symmetry only	Has reflective and rotational symmetry
			square

4 Draw the following shapes on the grid.

This shape has 4 straight sides.

It has no right angles.

It has 2 pairs of parallel sides.

This shape is a quadrilateral.

All sides are the same length.

It has 2 acute angles.

5 **Name the quadrilateral – a game for two players**

Player 1 draws a quadrilateral without player 2 seeing it.

Player 2 asks questions to identify the quadrilateral, for example, 'Does it have a line of symmetry?' Player 1 can only answer 'yes' or 'no'.

Keep a record of the number of questions. Score 1 point for every question needed to identify the quadrilateral correctly. Swap roles and repeat.
The winner is the player who needed the fewest questions after 5 rounds.

Record the questions you asked to identify the shape drawn by your partner.

Draw the shape.

Unit 1C: Geometry and problem solving, **Unit 3C:** Geometry and problem solving
CPM framework 6Gs1, 6Gs3, 6Pt4; Teacher's Resource 8.1, 34.1

Using coordinates

Remember

The convention for using coordinates is that (−3, −2) describes a point found by starting from the origin (0, 0) and moving three squares to the left and two squares down.

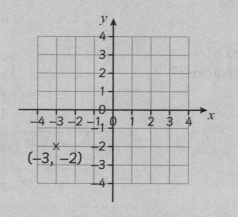

(−3, −2)

You will need:
resource 11, page 91, for activities 5 and 6

Vocabulary
coordinates, axis, origin

1   The points A and B are plotted on a coordinate grid.

Plot the point C (2, −4) on the grid.

Find the coordinates of the point D so that ABCD is a square.

_____

> **Hint:** Be sure to follow the convention: across before up or down.

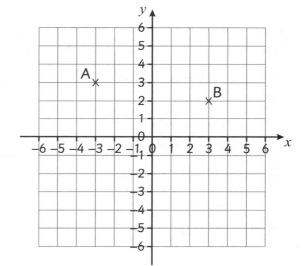

2   Triangle ABC is translated 4 squares left and 3 squares down.

What are the coordinates of the vertices of the triangle in its new position?

_____

> **Hint:** Translation is a movement on a grid. See page 21.

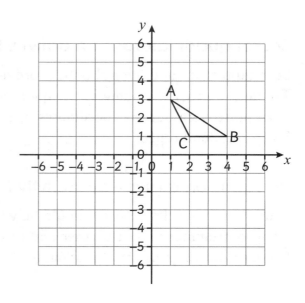

Unit 1C: Geometry and problem solving, Unit 3C: Geometry and problem solving
CPM framework 6Gp1; Teacher's Resource 10.1, 34.2

79

3 Here are three triangles on a coordinate grid.

What are the coordinates of the next triangle in the sequence?

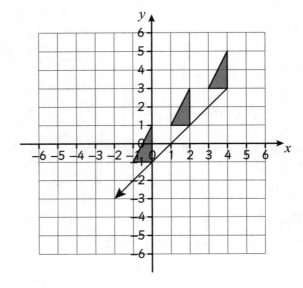

4 A line is drawn on a coordinate grid.

(−4, 3) are coordinates of a point on the line.

Circle all the coordinates of other points on the line:

(−2, 1)   (2, −3)   (−1, 0)

(1, 2)   (−3, 2)   (−3, −4)

(−5, 4)   (1, −2)

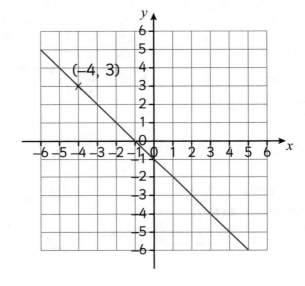

5 **Secret quadrilateral – an activity for pairs**

Secretly plot a quadrilateral on a coordinate grid on the resource.
Tell your partner the name of the quadrilateral and the coordinates of three of the vertices.
They must work out the coordinates of the fourth vertex.
Swap roles and repeat.

6 **Polygons on a grid – an activity for pairs**

Draw a polygon. Its vertices should be whole number coordinates.
Swap coordinates with a partner and draw each other's polygons.
Do your drawings match the original?

Unit 1C: Geometry and problem solving, **Unit 3C:** Geometry and problem solving
CPM framework 6Gp1; Teacher's Resource 10.1, 34.2

1	2	3	4
5	6	7	8
9	10	12	14
15	16	18	20
21	24	25	27
30	32	36	40
42	0	5	0

45.2	4.52	4.25	54.2
25.4	2.54	42.4	5.42
2.52	25.2	42.2	4.22
52.4	5.24	4.54	45.4
24.5	5.45	54.5	44.5

Resource 3
Sum to 10

Cut out the two sets of cards.

5.4 + ☐ = 10	6.3 + ☐ = 10	7.8 + ☐ = 10	8.9 + ☐ = 10
4.6 + ☐ = 10	3.4 + ☐ = 10	2.7 + ☐ = 10	1.9 + ☐ = 10
9.2 + ☐ = 10	0.8 + ☐ = 10	3.14 + ☐ = 10	4.72 + ☐ = 10
4.14 + ☐ = 10	5.72 + ☐ = 10	3.42 + ☐ = 10	4.42 + ☐ = 10
6.38 + ☐ = 10	7.38 + ☐ = 10	8.38 + ☐ = 10	5.14 + ☐ = 10

4.6	3.7	2.2	1.1	5.4
6.6	7.3	8.1	0.8	9.2
6.86	5.28	5.86	4.28	6.58
5.58	3.62	2.62	1.62	4.86

Resource 4
Compare numbers

Grid

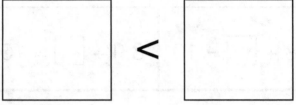

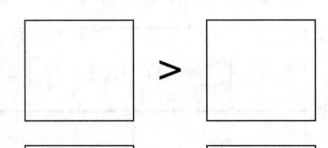

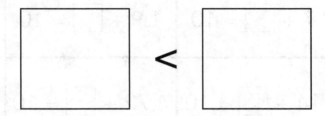

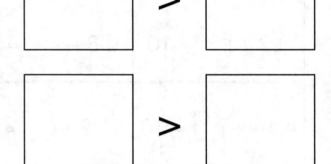

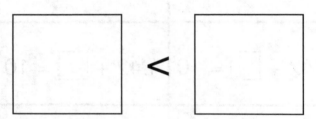

Cut out the 12 cards.

0	–1	2	–2
3	4	–4	–5
–6	–7	–8	–9

Photocopiable resources

Original material © Cambridge University Press 2016

Resource 5
Division match

Cut out the cards.

$36 \div 5$	$30 \div 4$	$31 \div 4$	$76 \div 10$	$34 \div 5$
$7\frac{1}{5}$	$7\frac{1}{2}$	$7\frac{3}{4}$	$7\frac{3}{5}$	$6\frac{4}{5}$
7.2	7.5	7.75	7.6	6.8
$27 \div 4$	$26 \div 4$	$42 \div 5$	$32 \div 4$	$87 \div 10$
$6\frac{3}{4}$	$6\frac{1}{2}$	$8\frac{2}{5}$	$8\frac{1}{4}$	$8\frac{7}{10}$
6.75	6.5	8.4	8.25	8.7

Photocopiable resources

Resource 6
Multiplication golf

In the game of golf, players hit a ball with a club. Different numbered golf clubs hit balls different distances when hit with different strengths. The score sheet gives the number of holes to be played and the distance the ball has to travel for each hole.

Example: If a player selects club number 2 and chooses to use strength 6 the ball will travel a distance of 12 (2 × 6). If this distance is not enough to get the ball to the hole, the player may hit again with a different club if necessary.

Clubs 2 5 8		Strengths 1 6 7	
Hole	**Length**	**Distance travelled each stroke**	**Number of strokes**
8	44	5 x 6 = 30 2 x 7 = 14	2

The object of the game is to get the ball into the hole with the minimum number of strokes.

Multiplication golf score sheet

Clubs 2 5 8		Strengths 1 6 7	
Hole	**Length**	**Distance travelled each stroke**	**Number of strokes**
1	48		
2	73		
3	57		
4	81		
5	98		
6	26		
7	90		
8	44		
9	159		
		Total	

Resource 7
Mode and range jigsaw

Cut out the jigsaw pieces. Reassemble by matching each data set to the correct mode and range.

2, 4, 3, 4, 4 1, 2, 9, 2, 8	mode = 2, range = 9 6, 7, 6, 8, 5 8, 4, 8, 4, 8	mode = 8, range = 4 0, 4, 0, 4, 4
mode = 4, range = 3 6, 2, 9, 7, 4 3, 13, 15, 3, 8	mode = 6, range = — 3 mode = 6, range = 55 10, 3, 7, 6, 3	mode = 4, range = 4 6, 7, 5, 6, 9 6, 3, 7, 5, 3
mode = 3, range = 12 4, 7, 4, 8, 11 9, 5, 6, 5, 8	mode = 3, range = 7 mode = 4, range = 7 6, 3, 11, 6, 7	mode = 3, range = 4 1, 2, 7, 4, 2 7, 5, 6, 7, 4
mode = 5, range = 4 2, 4, 9, 7, 4	mode = 6, range = 8 mode = 4, range = 5 7, 2, 3, 7, 4	mode = 7, range = 3 mode = 7, range = 5

Photocopiable resources

Resource 8
Fraction pairs

Cut out the cards.

$3\frac{1}{2}$	$4\frac{2}{3}$	$5\frac{1}{4}$	$2\frac{1}{3}$
$4\frac{3}{4}$	$2\frac{3}{5}$	$1\frac{4}{5}$	$2\frac{2}{5}$
$\frac{7}{2}$	$\frac{14}{3}$	$\frac{21}{4}$	$\frac{7}{3}$
$\frac{19}{4}$	$\frac{13}{5}$	$\frac{9}{5}$	$\frac{12}{5}$

Resource 9
Matching fractions and decimals

Cut out the cards.

one half	one hundredth	one third	one quarter
one fifth	two tenths	three tenths	four tenths
ten hundredths	one half	$\dfrac{5}{10}$	$\dfrac{1}{100}$
$\dfrac{1}{3}$	$\dfrac{1}{10}$	$\dfrac{1}{4}$	$\dfrac{1}{2}$
$\dfrac{4}{10}$	$\dfrac{10}{100}$	$\dfrac{2}{10}$	$\dfrac{3}{10}$

Resource 10
Matching ratio and proportion statements

Cut out the cards.

For every 2 circles there is 1 square	In every 3 shapes there are 2 circles	There is 1 square to every 2 circles
For every 2 circles there are 3 squares	In every 5 shapes there are 2 circles	There are 3 squares to every 2 circles
For every 4 circles there is 1 square	In every 5 shapes there is 1 square	There is 1 square to every 4 circles
For every 3 circles there is 1 square	In every 4 shapes there is 1 square	There is 1 square to every 3 circles

Resource 11
Coordinates

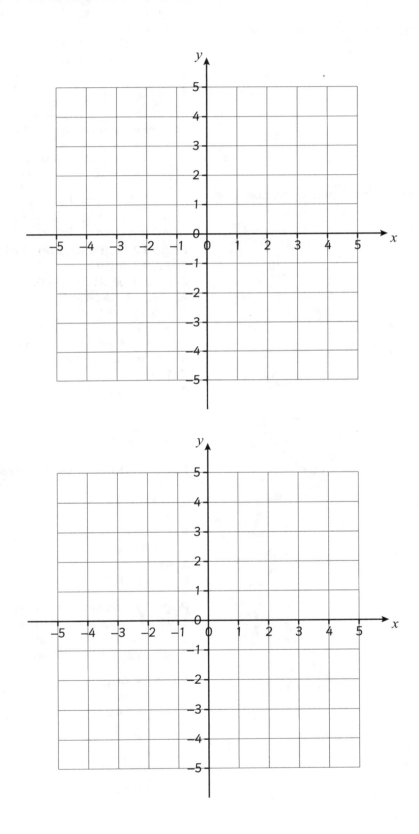

Answers

Page 4 Place value, ordering and rounding (whole numbers)

1 694 502

six hundred and ninety four thousand, five hundred and two

6 hundred thousand

2 90 009

3 35, 606 000, 1000, 100, 4800, 901

4 1000, 5000, 52 000, 515 000

5 9960

7 3654

8 =, >, <

9 approximately 7000

10 A

Page 7 Multiples, factors, odd and even numbers

1 There are alternative ways of working out the answers

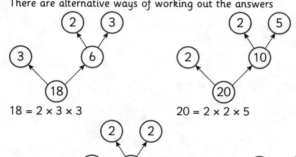

$18 = 2 \times 3 \times 3$ $20 = 2 \times 2 \times 5$

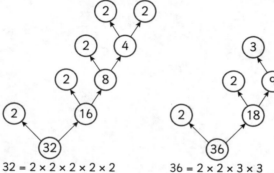

$32 = 2 \times 2 \times 2 \times 2 \times 2$ $36 = 2 \times 2 \times 3 \times 3$

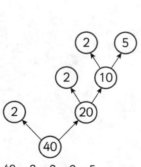

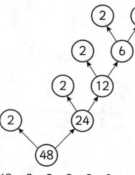

$40 = 2 \times 2 \times 2 \times 5$ $48 = 2 \times 2 \times 2 \times 2 \times 3$

2 Game

3 odd, even, even

4 common multiples for 4 and 6: 12, 24, 36

common multiples for 2 and 5: 10, 20

common multiples for 3 and 4: 12, 24

common multiples for 4 and 7: 28

common multiples for 3 and 10: 30

Page 10 Prime numbers

1 The prime numbers remaining are: 2, 3, 5, 7, 11, 13, 17, 19, 23, 29, 31, 37, 41, 43, 47, 53, 59, 61, 67, 71, 73, 79, 83, 89, 97

2 7 and 2, 13 and 3

3 Number 1: 5 or 13

Number 2: 5, 13 or 17

4 P

5

8	4	6	8	13
3	13	12	17	15
1	11	15	5	5
15	12	5	1	2
11	14	16	4	11

Page 12 Multiplication strategies

1 7.2, 4.2, 0.7, 0.7

2 5600, 3600, 21 000, 24 000

4 697, 663, 406, 434

5 350, 720, 840, 210

$9 \times 8 = 18 \times 4 = 36 \times 2$

$3 \times 16 = 6 \times 8 = 12 \times 4 = 24 \times 2$

6 40×60 and 20×120

7 140, 44

8

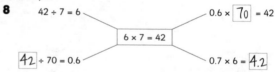

$42 \div 7 = 6$ $0.6 \times \boxed{70} = 42$

$6 \times 7 = 42$

$\boxed{42} \div 70 = 0.6$ $0.7 \times 6 = \boxed{4.2}$

Page 15 Number sequences

1 −20

2 2, 2.1; 3, $3\frac{1}{2}$; 999, 997

4 21

5 5, 10, 15

6 5, 8, 11; 6, 10

7 99

8 add 2 to the last number

Page 17 Drawing and measuring lines and angles

1 4.8 cm, 73 mm, 42° and 48°, sum = 90°

3 $a = 125°$, $b = 95°$, $c = 140°$

4 8.5 cm/85 mm; 9 cm/90 mm; 10.5 cm/105 mm; 7 cm/70 mm

Page 19 Angles

1 180°

2 $a = 144°$, $b = 115°$, $c = 110°$, $d = 30°$

Answers

Page 21 Transformations on a grid

1
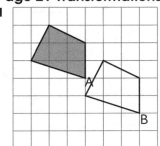

2 3 squares to the left and 1 square up

3
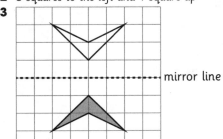
mirror line

4
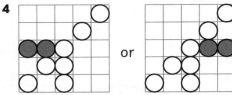
or

5
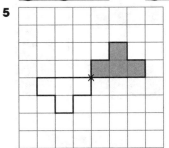

6
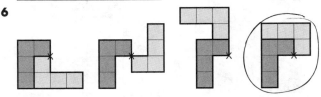

Page 23 3D shapes

1

	Number of faces	Number of vertices	Number of edges
tetrahedron	4	4	6
octahedron	8	6	12

2 square-based pyramid

3 C

4
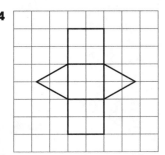

5
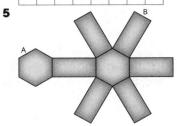

hexagonal prism

Page 25 Numbers in Ancient Greece

1
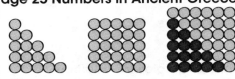

2 15

3 1, 4, 9, 16, 25, 36, 49, 64, 81, 100

4 16

5 15

6 1 + 9 = 10   4 + 16 = 20

7 Pattern of odd numbers starting at 3

Page 27 The decimal system

1 7 tenths, 5 hundredths

4 1 metre, $5.40

Page 30 Addition and subtraction of decimals

1
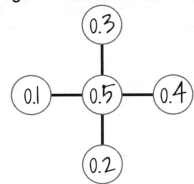

Other arrangements possible but 0.5 must be in the centre.

2 5.4, 1.9, 4.14, 6.38

Answers

3 0.51 + 0.49 = 1
0.26 + 0.74 = 1
0.37 + 0.63 = 1
0.92 + 0.08 = 1
0.75 + 0.25 = 1
0.89 + 0.11 = 1
0.24 + 0.76 = 1
0.19 + 0.81 = 1
4 68, 6.8, 0.68
138, 13.8, 1.38
5 95.9, 48.7, 86.3
22.2, 14.8, 2.2

Page 32 Positive and negative numbers
1 −4°C, −3°C, −1°C, 0°C, 1°C, 6°C, 8°C
2 days
4
−4°C
2 8, 8, 5, 5
3 2, −1, −4
4 0, 0
5 3, −1, −3, −4, −7
6 8°C, 8°, 4°C

Page 34 Mental strategies for addition and subtraction
1 820   240
610   610
8.2   2.4
1.28   0.15
11.1   0.54
3.7   0.28

2

Calculation	Strategy	✓ or ✗	Correct version
13.4 − 6.8	13.4 − 7 − 0.2	✗	13.4 − 7 + 0.2
12.4 + 3.9	12.4 + 4 − 0.1	✓	
31.2 − 9.9	31.2 − 10 + 0.1	✓	

3 7.4 − 0.1 = 7.3

Page 36 Divisibility rules
1

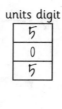

5 × table

units digit

5
0
5

2

units digit

4
8
2
6
0
4

4 × table

204, 124, 244

Page 38 Division
1 85
4 $20\frac{4}{5}$ or 20.8
$26\frac{3}{4}$ or 26.75
$94\frac{1}{2}$ or 94.5
$59\frac{1}{2}$ or 59.5
5 a) 21 b) 63

Page 40 Multiplication
2 8, 720
3 140, 280
4 13 × 17 = 136 + 68 + 17 = 221
5 68 × 17 = 1190 − 34 = 1156
6 27 × 32 = 288 × 3 = 864
7

¹1	5	3	9		³7	2
4			⁴4	2	2	4
⁵4	5	⁶1	8		1	
4		4		⁷1	2	6	⁸5
	⁹2	9	¹⁰2	8		0
¹¹1	5	6	8	¹²5	1	2
	6		¹³6	2	8	4
¹⁴1	5	4	8	¹⁵5	4	

Page 42 Time
1 60, 24, 7, 4, 12, 100, 1000
2 12:15
3 16:00
4 2 hours 45 minutes
5 40 minutes
6 D, B, C, A   DCBA
7 11:17
8 3 hours 50 minutes

Answers

9

	Start time	Finish time	Time taken
Amira	10:30	11:55	1 hour 25 minutes
Bimla	10:35	12:05	1 hour 30 minutes
Conrad	10:40	12:08	1 hour 28 minutes
Delroy	10:45	12:20	1 hour 35 minutes

10 minutes

Page 44 Area and perimeter

1 12 squares
3 C and D
4 length 6 cm, area = 12 cm²
5 perimeter = 30 cm, area = 50 cm²
6 116 cm², 71 cm²

Page 46 Using data

1

miles	25	50	72.5	100
kilometres	40	80	120	165

2 $150, (actual £37.50) accept £35 – £40
3 60, 33

Page 48 Mode and range

66
67, 102
10, 33, week 2
6 secs, 32 secs

Page 50 Mean and median

1 32
2 Any whole number greater or equal to 7
3 35
4 5
5 7, 6
6 20, 21, 18

Page 52 Statistics in everyday life

1 mode = 6, range = 6
2 The intermediate points have no value
3 2
4 True. 23 students attended the club each Wednesday
Insufficient information. Different students could attend each week

Page 54 Probability

3 2 or 4 in each cell.
4 1, 3, 2, 2, 2, 2, 2, 2 or 1, 1, 3, 3, 2, 2, 2, 2
5 1 and 2
There are four 3s and four other numbers
6 certain, impossible, even chance

Page 56 Multiplication

1 2652, 2881, 5917, 1564
2 676 passengers, $312

Page 58 Division

1 21, 14, 19, 38

2 Calculations for jigsaw:
$667 \div 23 = 29$
$364 \div 14 = 26$
$837 \div 31 = 27$
$360 \div 24 = 15$
$532 \div 19 = 28$
$986 \div 34 = 29$
$378 \div 27 = 14$
$540 \div 15 = 36$
$672 \div 28 = 24$
$972 \div 27 = 36$
$638 \div 29 = 22$
$902 \div 22 = 41$
$962 \div 37 = 26$
$561 \div 17 = 33$
$448 \div 16 = 28$
$533 \div 13 = 41$
$875 \div 35 = 25$

Page 60 The laws of arithmetic

1 355, 342
2 201, 744
3 215, 244
4 $3 \times (8 + 2) = 30$
$(9 - 4) \times 2 = 10$
5

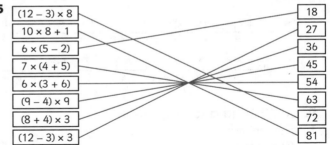

6 11, 9

Page 62 Fractions

1 $\frac{2}{8}, \frac{4}{8}, \frac{6}{8}$
$\frac{3}{4} = \frac{6}{8}$ so $\frac{3}{4}$ is larger
2 $\frac{1}{5}, \frac{2}{5}, \frac{3}{5}, \frac{4}{5}$
4 $\frac{3}{4}$
5 $\frac{4}{5} = \frac{8}{10}$ so $\frac{4}{5}$ is larger

Page 64 Mixed numbers and improper fractions

1 $3\frac{3}{5}, 1\frac{7}{8}, 5\frac{3}{4}, 3\frac{1}{5}$
2 $\frac{35}{8}, \frac{25}{3}, \frac{23}{4}, \frac{20}{3}$

3

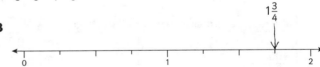

Answers

5 $1\frac{2}{3}$, $3\frac{1}{3}$
7 8

8 $3\frac{1}{2}$, $4\frac{3}{4}$

Page 66 Fractions and decimals

1
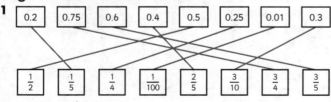

3 one third = $\frac{1}{3}$ = $0.\dot{3}$

one quarter = $\frac{1}{4}$ = 0.25

4 $\frac{1}{2}$ + 0.1 + 0.40 (do not allow the addition of two numbers)

5 $\frac{3}{5}$ and $\frac{5}{100}$

Page 68 Percentages

1
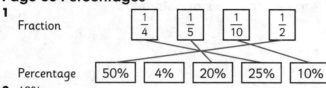

2 40%

3
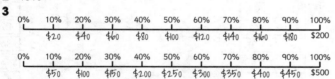

Page 70 Ratio and proportion

1 25 protractors
2 16 white flowers
3 10 kiwi fruit
4 900 grams

Page 72 Metric and imperial measures

1
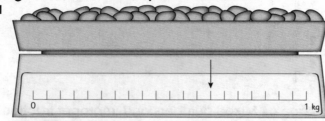

2

Kilograms and grams					
1 kg	0.5 kg	0.1 kg	0.001 kg	0.75 kg	0.7 kg
1000 g	500 g	100 g	1 g	750 g	700 g

Metres, centimetres and millimetres					
1 m	0.001 m	0.5 m	0.75 m	0.4 m	0.25 m
100 cm	0.1 cm	50 cm	75 cm	40 cm	25 cm
1000 mm	1 mm	500 mm	750 mm	400 mm	250 mm

3

3 miles	⟨3 kilometres⟩
⟨4 pints⟩	4 litres
5 pounds	⟨5 grams⟩
6 inches	⟨6 centimetres⟩

4 8.8 gallons
5 Alternative answers including:
2 × 5 ounces = 300 grams but 10 ounces = 270 grams

Page 74 Time zones, timetables and calendars

1 33 days
2 20th December
3 09:10, 11:05
4 8 a.m. or 08:00
3 p.m or 15:00
5 2 hours 35 minutes, 2 hours 43 minutes, 2 hours 30 minutes,
2 hours 36 minutes, 2 hours 37 minutes, 2 hours 45 minutes
165 minutes
A, C, D, E
6 12:30, 21:00, 16:00

Page 77 2D shapes

1
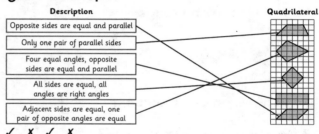

2 ✓ ✗ ✓ ✗

3

Has reflective symmetry only	Has rotational symmetry only	Has reflective and rotational symmetry
rectangle kite	parallelogram	square rhombus

4 a parallelogram and a rhombus

Page 79 Using coordinates

1 Plot C at (2, −4), D (−4, −3)
2 (−3, 0) (0, −2) (−2, −2)
3 (−2, −3) (−3, −3) (−2, −1)
4 (−2, 1) (2, −3) (−1, 0) (−3, 2) (−5, 4) (1, −2)